FINDING FAMILIES

SAGE HUMAN SERVICES GUIDES, VOLUME 7

SAGE HUMAN SERVICES GUIDES

*a series of books edited by ARMAND LAUFFER and published in coopera-
tion with the Continuing Education Program in the Human Services of the
University of Michigan School of Social Work.*

FINDING FAMILIES

An Ecological Approach to Family Assessment in Adoption

A Project CRAFT Publication
by Ann Hartman

Volume 7
SAGE HUMAN SERVICES GUIDES

Published in cooperation with the North American Center on Adoption, Inc. and the Continuing Education Program in the Human Services of the University of Michigan School of Social Work

SAGE PUBLICATIONS   Beverly Hills/London

SAGE PUBLICATIONS, INC.
275 South Beverly Drive
Beverly Hills, California 90212

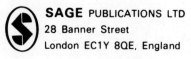

SAGE PUBLICATIONS LTD
28 Banner Street
London EC1Y 8QE, England

Printed in the United States of America

Library of Congress Cataloging in Publication Data

Hartman, Ann.
  Finding families.

  (Sage human services guides ; v. 7)
  Bibliography: p.
  1. Adoption—United States. 2. Family social work—
United States. I. Title.
HV875.H28   362.7'34'0973   78-26537
ISBN 0-8039-1216-1

SECOND PRINTING

CONTENTS

ABOUT THIS BOOK

Finding Families is Volume 7 of the *Sage Human Services Guides* published by Sage Publications and developed by the Continuing Education Program in the Human Services of the University of Michigan School of Social Work. Professor Armand Lauffer is Series Editor.

The following guides were developed by the staff of Project CRAFT (Curriculum Resources for Adoption and Foster Care Training):

Resources: For Child Placement and Other Human Services by Armand Lauffer with contributions by Bonnie Carlson, Kayla Conrad, and Lynn Nybell (Volume 6, SHSG)

Finding Families: An Ecological Approach to Family Assessment in Adoption by Ann Hartman (Volume 7, SHSG)

No Child Is Unadoptable: A Reader on Adoption of Children with Special Needs edited by Sallie R. Churchill, Bonnie Carlson, and Lynn Nybell (Volume 8, SHSG)

Work on these guides was funded through a grant by the Edna McConnell Clark Foundation. The concepts in each were tested with seasoned practitioners and administrators from child welfare agencies throughout the United States and Canada. A subsequent grant from the Children's Bureau, U.S. Department of Health, Education and Welfare, facilitated the dissemination of these materials.

INTRODUCTION

Finding Families, together with its three companion monographs, has been developed as a part of Project CRAFT, an ongoing training project conducted at The University of Michigan School of Social Work. Founded with the purpose of developing leaders in adoption and foster care practice, Project CRAFT (Curriculum Resources in Adoption and Foster Care Training) was initiated through the support of a grant from the Edna McConnell Clark Foundation. Its sponsorship has been expanded to include federal, state, and local agencies. Project CRAFT owes much to the continuing encouragement of the Clark Foundation and its executive vice-president, Peter Forsythe.

Although all four volumes are directed toward developing increased knowledge and skill in child welfare practice, we hope that they may also be of use to human service practitioners in other areas of service.

Each volume has benefited, to some degree, from exposure to graduates of the CRAFT Leadership Training Program, and to the fifty social work educators who attended the faculty workshops for social work educators. The testing out with practitioners and educators has been invaluable in keeping the materials intimately related to the needs of those working in adoption and foster care.

Project CRAFT has benefited from the encouragement and support provided by Elizabeth Cole and other staff members of the North American Center on Adoption, co-sponsor of these volumes. The project has also been enriched through interaction with its sister projects at Columbia University School of Social Work, headed by Mary Funnyé Goldson, and at the University of Southern California School of Social Work, headed by Carol Williams.

Finally, a personal word of acknowledgement is in order to those who contributed to the development of this volume on family assessment. It is impossible to identify all of the sources of the ideas that are developed here, but some can be singled out. My long association with Carel Germain of the University of Connecticut has been a major influence in the development of the ecological perspective. The translation of this perspective into social work practice with and in behalf of families and children has been enriched by my ongoing collaboration in this area with Joan Laird of Eastern Michigan University.

Concerning the development of the assessment tools, the EcoMap was first developed by the author as a part of my involvement in the Child Welfare Learning Laboratory project at The University of Michigan. The use of the genogram has come out of the family therapy movement, but it was Fernando Colon of The University of Michigan whose work made me aware of the rich potential of this tool in adoption and foster care practice. Kitty La Parriere of the Nathan Ackerman Family Therapy Institute first exposed me to the technique of family sculpture.

I am grateful to Gloria Thomas and Sylvia Grey who gave me the opportunity through the Temporary Foster Care Project of the State of Michigan Department of Social Services to test out the assessment model with biofamilies of children in care and to the line workers and supervisors who took the tools into the field.

The Clark Foundation has made possible the actual preparation of the monograph through the provision of the required time and supports.

I want to thank my readers, Professor Hilda Arndt of Louisiana State University School of Social Welfare, and Louise Curtin of the Maryland Social Service Administration. Their investment of time and their thoughtful criticism contributed much to the final volume.

I want to acknowledge the contribution of the staff of CRAFT: Lynn Nybell worked with me on the original EcoMap and was particularly helpful in developing guidelines for training; Christine Stilwell did the graphics and preliminary typing; Joan Eadie typed the manuscript, and Ellen Saalberg did a masterful job of editing.

Finally, I want to thank Armand Lauffer who initially directed Project CRAFT and whose enthusiasm and energy got us going and kept us going.

Ann Arbor, 1979   *Ann Hartman*

Chapter 1

PERMANENCE FOR CHILDREN

Child welfare services are going through a period of rapid, perhaps even revolutionary change. In every area of service to children and families, the growing demand for permanence for all children is heard. Foster care and child protective agencies are focusing their resources on work with biological families toward the return of children home and the support of the family unit. When it can be demonstrated that families are going to be unable to provide permanent care for their children, agencies are making every effort to free children for adoption so that permanent plans may be made.

Adoption programs increasingly focus on finding permanent homes for the thousands of children in "temporary" care who have, in the past, been defined as "hard to place." The very term "hard to place children" is being questioned as it locates the problem within the child rather than within the dysfunctional service system. This system has tended to define adoption and adoptive homes in a way that excludes all but a very young, generally white child, free of any kind of physical or psychological handicap or even correctable condition.

These changes in the delivery of services to children make demands on agencies for innovative and creative practice and for a willingness to take risks. They also require a continuing effort to expand knowledge and enhance skills in practice situations that are more and more complex. For example, the current conviction in adoption practice that every child is "adoptable" leads to a changing view of the total adoptive process, including new approaches to recruitment and assessment, preparation of children and parents, and post-adoption services.

This volume is presented in the hope that it will be useful to social workers in adoption practice as they enhance their knowledge and expand their skills, particularly in the complex family assessment process that is so central to adoption practice.

WHAT THE BOOK IS ALL ABOUT

A model of family assessment is presented in a step-by-step fashion. This model is conceived of as shared process that takes place between adoptive applicants and adoption workers. The goal of this shared process is creative planning around placement.

Growing out of an ecological systems perspective that views individuals and families as open systems, deeply immersed in their environments, the assessment model includes specific assessment tools that translate the ecological perspective into practice. These tools attempt to capture for observation and exploration the complex dynamics of the family system in space and through time.

The practice portion of the volume begins with a discussion of the first phase of work with adoptive applicants. Contracting is explored with special reference to its relevance to the adoptive applicant's role in the adoption process. The three dimensions of family assessment are presented, the assessment tools are described, and use of the tools is illustrated with case materials.

The first tool presented is the EcoMap, which enables the worker and the adoptive applicants to picture the family in relation to its world. The EcoMap portrays the sources of support, strain, conflict, and gratification that exist for the family in its life space.

The family is a living system that has developed through time and has a life history as individual and characteristic as a fingerprint. The second assessment tool demonstrated is the genogram that charts the family history through time.

Third, we look at the family system itself as a system. Information around boundaries, role, communication, power, and change is identified and examined, particularly in terms of relevance to adoption. Family diagramming and family sculpture are presented as ways of simulating and gaining understanding of the family as a system.

After a brief look at some aspects of decision-making and the relevance of the systems assessment tools to post-adoption services, the volume concludes with a brief guide concerning methods of teaching the family assessment tools to staff development and other training groups.

Before moving on to the presentation of the assessment model, and in order to be consistent with our ecological perspective, we must pause to at least sketch out in broad terms the context within which adoption practice and particularly the assessment process is to be understood. Just as the family is immersed in and impacted by its environment in space and through time, so has this social invention, adoption, been formed by its history and so now responds to the currents of the larger society of which it is a part.

We first describe a few of the major issues that currently have a major impact on adoption practice. We then examine the historical development of the "home finding" process, particularly as this process is expressive of the values of the time and the available or preferred bodies of knowledge and theory.

CURRENT ISSUES IN ADOPTION PRACTICE

Perhaps the major issue in determining the cause and nature of adoption practice is expressed in the question, "Who is the primary beneficiary of this service?" The most important shift in adoption practice in recent years has been the slow and halting change from viewing adoption as primarily a service for childless couples to redefining adoption as dedicated to finding families for children who need them. This shifting emphasis alters the face of adoption.

The following anecdote was reported at the 1884 National Conference of Charities and Corrections and demonstrates the emphasis on serving parents:

> Then there comes some little person of seven years who does not suit the place, because the child of the family who died had fair hair and blue eyes and a very bright intelligence. Little Josie has dark hair and is somewhat plain and backward. She will be sent to the primary school to wait for another chance, and meantime will be trained in housework, sewing, and studies and better fitted for going out again. The applicants go to the Primary School, choose a fair haired child with a view to adoption and are well content.[1]

The primary recipient of this service is clearly the adoptive family. The effort is to help the couple complete their family, to help them find a substitute for the lost child. As we review the emphasis in adoptive programs since that time, it would appear that there continues to be in child placement practice, an emphasis on building "ideal" families rather than on meeting the needs of children.

A few observations may illustrate this emphasis. Until fairly recently, a large number of children have been considered "unadoptable" by virtue of age, racial background, or physical or mental disability. Agencies have tended to take the position that there were no adoptive homes available for these children. However, it is possible that it was the social agencies, not the prospective parents, that limited the definition of the "adoptable" child.

Henry Maas' study, in the late 1950s, of adoptive parents found that the "adoptive parents indicated more frequent parental tolerance for difference in adoptive children than the agencies' placement of adoptive children who were different made use of."[2] Sixty-one couples expressed willingness to accept a child with a physical handicap, but only thirty-five such children were placed with these couples. Sixty-three couples were willing to take a child of two or more, but only thirty-three older children were placed.

The practice of placing babies in "infant study homes" to make sure they were developing properly and had no "defects" before placement was widespread until recently. The effort was to guarantee that the child was adoptable, and this gave precedence over the possible harm to the child resulting from having to move or to the adoptive parent/child relationship through postponement. This concept of the "adoptable" child still seems to inform social workers' thinking and practice.

As recently as July 1975, in reporting a study of workers' judgement in the selection of adoptive families, Brown and Brieland conclude, "In view of the shortage of children for adoption, the judgement process must be made more objective and reliable."[3] In the face of discussions about this shortage, it happens that currently there are approximately 120,000 to 140,000 children in foster care who are legally free for adoption.[4] Clearly, when we talk about the shortage of children for adoption, we must have some image which does not include these children. Such an image may well spring from a continued conception of adoption as a process of finding babies for childless couples!

Running counter to this view has been a growing movement to find families for children, to redefine and expand the notion of the "adoptable child," to refuse to accept as inevitable that hundreds of thousands of children will grow up in "temporary" care, or as one young man said "to have no place to leave your high school yearbook when you go into the army."

A second issue that is having major impact on adoption practice is that of "open adoption" and the rights of children to information about and/or contact with their biological parents. This move toward the consideration of open adoption is a part of an awakening concern for and an appreciation of the importance of continuity to identity and personality development.

In response to this concern, some agencies are considering a variety of models of adoption that preserve ties to biological roots. Many agencies are becoming attentive to the meaning of relationships developed during temporary care arrangements and are attempting to plan ways of maintaining these ties—important sources of nurture and support.

A third major trend that is affecting all of social work practice and has major relevance for the family assessment process is the move toward participatory consumerism in all service delivery. No more are users or applicants for services willing to be passive while they are evaluated and acted upon. This participatory stance has particular relevance to the entire assessment process that is the primary focus of this volume. Assessment is seen here as an open process of active participation and sharing that takes place in an egalitarian atmosphere between the agency, the social worker, and the potential adoptive family.

A fourth major impact on adoption practice is the change in the American family itself. Family forms are altering and proliferating; the traditional family unit consisting of a working husband, a homemaker wife, and children is increasingly rare. Changes in the family require that agencies rethink their definitions and requirements in the search for families. The variety of children awaiting permanence requires a variety in the life styles and arrangements of families that may be found for these children. This variety is consistent with the pluralism that is fundamental in American life.

In attempting to develop a model of practice that is responsive to our pluralistic society, two definitions of the family are utilized. One, that is relatively simple, is the biological definition of the family as an extended network of blood kin. A second definition of the family relates to function and could be defined as any two people, at a minimum, be they two adults or an adult and a child, who share a commitment to one another of caring and continuity. In the case of a young child, this commitment is initially unilateral.

It is a commitment that may, but does not have to, be sanctioned by law as in marriage or adoption. In a sense, when those involved commit themselves to one another to perform the social, emotional, and economic functions generally performed by families, they are, in truth, a family. Such a definition includes traditional families, but it does not exclude the increasing variety of ways people come together to form families.

The final environmental change that has relevance to adoption practice is to be found in the altered intellectual climate. The impact of systems theory on the social sciences and the increased understanding of family systems, as developed particularly in the family therapy movements, make available a wealth of new insights to enrich our work with families and children. The family assessment model presented in this book draws upon an ecological systems perspective and upon family systems theory and attempts to translate these materials into concrete methods for adoption practice.

NOTES

1. Lesley, "Foundlings and Deserted Children," Proceedings of the National Conference of Charities and Corrections, 1884, p. 289.

2. Henry Maas, "The Successful Adoptive Parent Applicant," Social Work, 5:1 (January, 1960), p. 20.

3. Edwin Garth Brown and Donald Brieland, "Adoptive Screening, New Data, New Dilemmas," Social Work, 20:4 (July, 1975), p. 295.

4. Personal communication to the author from Child Welfare League of America, January, 1978.

Chapter 2

VALUES AND NORMS: A BIRD'S EYE VIEW OF THE HISTORY OF HOMEFINDING

Perhaps no area of adoption practice has been more obviously an expression of the value positions of the time than the area that forms the central focus of this volume, the assessment process or "the home study."

It is understandable that this should be so. The task of conducting a home study has been an "evaluative" one of measuring families against norms in an effort to make a decision as to whether a particular home is a "good" home, and whether a particular set of persons will be "good" parents. Through the careful selection of adoptive families, social workers hoped to protect children and guarantee them what they need for growth and development.

THE IMPACT OF SOCIAL VALUES ON ADOPTION PRACTICE

A social historian interested in studying changing American values and world view could gain quite a perspective simply by tracing changing definitions of a good home for children. In a sense, values that might be quite hidden in some areas of social life and thought get operationalized in standards and practices when selecting homes for children.

Those currently involved in finding and assessing families for children in need of permanent plans are expressing values, perhaps unknown to them, in the selection process. Some of these values relate to the worker's own personal biases and family experiences. Other values may well be expressions of the socialization process workers are exposed to as they become a member of the social work profession. No matter what the source, every effort should be made to surface and to examine these values and assumptions. A review of the history of homefinding and the changing values that have been implicit in our evaluations may aid in this values clarification process.

THE BEGINNINGS OF SUBSTITUTE FAMILY PLACEMENTS

The first extensive program for the placement of children in substitute homes was launched in 1854 by Charles Loring Brace and his colleagues at the Children's Aid Society, when forty-six New York City street children were transported to Michigan and placed in farm homes. In the following seventy-five years, 51,000 children were placed in the midwest by that agency alone. Brace described the method of selection and placement as follows:

> We formed little companies of immigrants, and after thoroughly cleaning and clothing them, put them under a competent agent and first selecting a village where there was a call or opening for such a party, we dispatched them to the place. The farming community having been duly notified, there was usually a dense crowd of people at the station, awaiting the arrival of the youthful travelers.
>
> The sight of the little company of the children of misfortune always touched the hearts of a population naturally generous. They were soon billeted around among the citizens and the following day a public meeting was called ... and a committee appointed of leading citizens. The agent then addressed the assembly, stating the benevolent objectives of the society, and something of the history of the children.
>
> The sight of their worn faces was a most pathetic enforcement of his arguments. People who were childless came forward to adopt children; others who had not intended to take any into their families were induced to apply for them; and many who really wanted the children's labor pressed forward to obtain it.[1]

The value premises underlying this practice were clear. First, as indicated by the title of Brace's report of his work, *The Dangerous Classes of New York,* this program was developed to protect the cities from gangs of unattached youth that would otherwise grow into a "class of paupers and criminals." Further, as to the selection of homes, the romanticizing of the agrarian life as opposed to the evils of the city was clear. Fresh air, hard outdoor work, the wholesomeness of farm life—these were seen as "good" for children.

Many agricultural metaphors were used as devoted child placement workers spoke of "transplanting" children to "good soil." Of considerable importance was the fact that children on the farm were an economic asset, not a liability. By the 1880s, concern about what was happening to children so placed was mounting. Part of this concern arose from reports of abuse, neglect, and exploitation suffered by the children.

There was criticism that "many vicious and depraved children are sent out by the Society; that they are hastily placed in homes without proper inquiry and are often ill used, ... and that a large portion turned out badly, swelling the ranks of pauperism and crime."[2] There were also objections from the Catholic church because many of the children placed were of Catholic heritage while the farm homes to which they were sent in Michigan, Ohio, and Indiana were those of protestant families.

THE HOME STUDY

The growing concern about what was happening to children in foster care and adoption and the increased interest in "scientific charity" led to the beginning of foster home investigations. Charles W. Birtwell, who became "Outdoor Worker" to the Boston Children's Aid Society in 1886 took the leadership in developing formal home studies, including office interviews, home visits, and investigation of references.

The study was guided by a series of questions including demographic data, "physical condition, church membership and attendance, character, disposition, habits of each member of the family," size of house, land, livestock, "previous experience in the care and training of children," the motive for taking a child.[3]

Not only were families "investigated," but the notion of "matching" began to appear.

> In all cases where adoption of a child is sought by childless parents, too much care cannot be taken by the visitor to consider the personal equation. ... It is of real value to fit the right peg in the right hole. A child that may be a torment in one family would be a blessing in another. And for children of promise, promising parents should be sought.[4]

The effort became one of finding a child for a family that was as close as possible to the child the couple might have had were they the biological parents. The notion of family building as a service to childless couples began to be entrenched in adoption practice.

Adoption as a service and as a practice became professionalized as social work became a profession. Identified areas of knowledge, skill, and function began to characterize the social work practitioner and the adoptive and foster homefinder. Dorothy Hutchinson's volume *In Quest of Foster Parents* published in 1943, became the bible for homefinders and expressed certain definitions of a "good" family.

"Normality" wrote Hutchinson, "is something that is hard to define, yet easy to see and feel."[5] Some definition of normality was attempted. "These people have made reasonably satisfactory adjustments to the demands of everyday life. They can hold a job, make and keep friends, marry and enjoy love, and meet the common stresses of life."[6] Such evaluative measures were reinforced by being given the sanction of the "expert."

A rereading of this volume surfaces other conceptions of the potential foster/adoptive family. Perhaps most dramatic is the implicit assumption that emerges throughout the book that *the* applicant is the potential foster mother. Not only is the term "foster mother" used almost exclusively throughout, instead of "foster parent," but in the description of the home study, the initial interview is almost always with the potential foster or adoptive mother. The sexism of the period is evident in the implicit view that child care and parenting are the province of the woman. Hutchinson comments that "it is so usual as to be almost proverbial that foster fathers remain in the background during the application process,"[7] but she seems unaware that the very way the study is handled reinforces the exclusion of the father.

Sexism is further demonstrated in the following evaluation of a marital pair. "Both Mr. and Mrs. G. accept their respective masculine and feminine roles. The division of labor between them is a normal one, and they both like being what they are, a man and a woman."[8] The position is further illuminated as Hutchinson writes, "An office visit may be an economic measure if it eliminates at an early point an applicant who for obvious reasons cannot serve the agency and its work—for example, an aged woman of 70, a *single man,* or perhaps a woman who lives in too crowded quarters."[9]

Hutchinson's volume also gives evidence of the growing use of psychoanalytic theory as a base for social work practice. The writer emphasizes the importance of understanding the psychological significance of the wish for a child on an unconscious as well as a conscious level, and the need to distinguish between "healthy" and "neurotic" motives. This psychological orientation in "investigating" and approving adoptive homes culminated in the 1950s with the use of the Rorschach as a tool in adoption home studies![10] This, perhaps, represented the most extreme instance of the passive potential applicant being examined and evaluated by the professionals.

As we move closer to the present, it can still be instructive to attempt to discover what kind of norms and values about families, family life, and adoption emerge in standards relative to the acceptance of adoptive homes. The Child Welfare League of America has taken leadership in establishing these standards and as Henry Maas discovered in his study of adoptive applicants, this organization may have been quite successful in socializing social workers to accept a particular image of an adoptive family.

Maas reported that, "despite the variations among our nine communities in size and degree of urbanization, ethnic composition, economy, geography and history, the modal portrait or profiles of all the adoptive couples in each community were remarkably alike. It is as though adoption standards in the child welfare field transcended in their potency any relevant differences among the nine community cultures."[11]

THE MODAL ADOPTIVE COUPLE

The modal couple, as discovered in the Maas study, was in their mid-thirties, white, Protestant, middle-class, active church goers, and high school graduates. They were in good health, childless, unable to have children, and wanted an infant. They were described as stable, content in their marriage, and reported happy childhoods. In general, they were seen as "average Americans." It seems that this normative image also transcended the individual needs of different children.

As recently as 1975, Alfred Kadushin's text on child welfare services, which is used extensively in the training and socialization of prospective social workers, spelled out the usual requirements agencies have maintained for adoptive parents and, once again, a very specific picture emerges. The requirements describe a married couple between thirty-five and forty-five who can supply medical proof of infertility and are in good health.

Applicants must generally have a religious affiliation, financial stability, be emotionally healthy, and demonstrate a capacity for parenthood. They must have adjusted to sterility and have a happy marriage. An explanation of the couple's motivation for adoption and their attitudes toward illigitimacy is also suggested "since most of the children available for adoption are born out of wedlock."[12]

A similar description of the acceptable adoptive parent appears in the Child Welfare League of America 1972 Standards for Adoptive Service. Certainly, one thing becomes clear in reading these sets of standards; and that is, both describe some notion of an "ideal" or "average" American couple as acceptable or preferred applicants to adopt an infant.

But what of "different" children? What of the older child? The handicapped child? The child of mixed or minority racial heritage? There is a second set of standards often applied in the adoption homefinding process.

Kadushin describes it as "an accommodation which takes place between the adoptive applicant who fails to meet some of the generally accepted eligibility requirements and the social worker who is trying to place a child with special needs."[13]

This process is described by Kadushin in his study of adoptive parents of hard-to-place children. "Typically an applicant usually prefers to adopt a healthy, normal, white infant.... He recognizes that because he is over 40 years of age, or because he is in poor health, or because his wife is a member of a different religious faith, the social worker will probably consider him a marginally eligible applicant. In objectively appraising the chances to adopt a child who possesses the ideal qualities, the applicant comes to realize that in all probability a 'less desirable' child will be offered to him.... His willingness to compromise may be thought of as an expression of his desire to compensate for his marginal eligibility."[14] Kadushin refers to agencies' views that securing homes for "hard-to-place" children entailed a "regression from ideal standards."[15]

In her study of workers' perceptions of adoptive parents, Trudy Bradley found that private agencies tended to consider "less adequate" couples suitable for a hard-to-place child.[16] If hard-to-place children tend to be harder to raise on the basis that they are struggling with some special status, handicap, or problem, it seems ironic that they are placed with couples who, perhaps, have fewer resources.

EMPHASIS SHIFT: FROM THE FAMILY TO THE CHILD IN NEED

Agencies and programs that are moving with conviction into the field of adoption of the hard-to-place child, or better, children in need of adoptive homes, are attempting to redefine the picture of adoptive families. Dr. Leona Forbes, psychiatric consultant to the Los Angeles Department of Adoptions, has suggested eight adoptive parent characteristics important to a successful adoptive placement. "They are ability to work with the agency, to express tenderness, to arbitrate, to be tolerant, to live non-isolated lives, to be resiliant, to have a healthy ego that enables them to defer gratification, and a life style reciprocal to that of the child to be placed."[17]

Although an ideal psychological picture of the family continues to be stressed, the Los Angeles agency is attempting to reduce other obstacles. For instance, they recommend that policy "reduce objective standards about age, size of family, life styles, etc., to a minimum. The traditional ideal family does not necessarily meet the needs of a particular child."[18]

A 1978 *Policy Statement on Adoption* developed by the New York City Department of Social Services has been circulated to the many voluntary agencies from which the department purchases service. The statement requests that agencies "eliminate from their policy statements and adoption information strict and arbitrary criteria for judging characteristics of adoptive families."[19] In operationalizing this policy, the department directs that "the following shall no longer be reasons for rejection of inquirers and applicants or delay of the adoption study process:

1. A health problem that does not preclude parenting the child until young adulthood.

2. Single parent status.

3. Race and Ethnicity: Agencies should make an intensive effort to place children with persons of the child's own race or ethnic group. If the agency can demonstrate that substantial outreach efforts have failed to produce a suitable family of the child's own race or ethnic group, then a transracial adoption should be pursued.

4. Religion: When a family of the same religion is unavailable, a family of religion different from the child's must be considered.

5. Age: This must be viewed in conjunction with maturity, health, and possible existing relationships with the child.

6. Working status: Either or both parents may work, so long as provision can be made for adequate child care.

7. Income: Families with low incomes or receiving public assistance should be considered, especially since subsidy now can make it possible for a family to maintain an additional child without straining its ability to meet its other needs. The key issue is not the amount of income, but rather the family's ability to manage the resources it has.

8. Prior divorce.

9. Fertility: No proof of infertility shall be required.

10. Children: Families who have other biological, foster, or adoptive children should be considered.

11. Refusal by the applicant of a child that the agency previously offered.

12. Previous rejection of an applicant by another agency" (see note 19).

A brief review of the value-laden practice of finding homes for children gives substance to Ray Birdwhistell's theme in his provocative discussions of the American family. "As members of society," he writes, "the experts in that society become carriers of culture. If these experts and their knowledge are drawn from the section of the culture which has the greatest faith in the covert myths of that culture, it is likely that these myths, strengthened by personal experience, will dominate their investigatory or clinical decisions."[20]

How much has adoption practice been guided by myths, by the romanticizing of agrarian life, by sex role stereotyping, and most important, by biases concerning the ideal American family? How many children and families have we failed to serve because they did not fit the ideal?

How often have our value-laden definitions led adoptive parents to see themselves as "marginal" and, thereby, to see their adopted child as "less desirable." And perhaps the most powerful myth—a myth that grew from science and scientism—is the myth of the expert. The myth is that adoption workers can gather information about as complex a system as a human family and make reliable judgments and predictions about that system's capacity to rear a child.

What myths and internalized images of families do we continue to use as a yardstick with which to measure and guide our decision-making process? These images are so much a part of ourselves that they are hard to identify. As Leonard Duhl has commented, "Cognitive patterns such as our internal images of the family are difficult to recognize and to change. That which is constantly experienced as neutral to awareness, being so immersed in the identity, so 'egosyntonic,' . . . is rarely open to observation or challenge."[21]

A NEW APPROACH TO FAMILY ASSESSMENT

The approach to family assessment and decision-making in adoption practice presented in this volume is also a product of its time, current values, available knowledge base, and the particular biases of the writer. Some of these influences and positions may be identified here. Others are probably more obvious to the reader than to the writer, and yet others will emerge as outdated products of the seventies by readers in the future.

The following paragraphs are an attempt to identify the major stance taken in this volume's approach to family assessment in adoption practice.

First, and perhaps most important, the position is taken that the primary concern of an adoption program at this time is to find adoptive homes for the thousands of children waiting in "temporary" care and available for adoption. This priority grows out of the conviction that children need to have the security, continuity, identity base, and commitment of being a part of a family. In the task of finding families for children, the need of many adoptive parents for a child will also be served. However, clarity in terms of priority has considerable impact on every phase of adoption practice.

Second, an equalitarian, participatory approach is taken that defines the assessment process as a shared responsibility between social worker and adoptive family. As far as possible, the worker's role is to help members of the family gain more information and understanding about their family in space and through time, and to give them as much information as possible about adoption in general and about particular children to be considered. On the basis of an enhanced understanding of their family and knowledge about the demands of adoption, the worker helps the family make a decision about adoption and if they decide to adopt, helps them prepare.

Third, every effort is made to surface and to critically examine definitions or norms that are used to describe the "normal" or "healthy" family. Demographic characteristics, social and economic considerations, and particularly family structures are considered relevant only as they pertain to the needs of a specific child. In other words, the concept of a model of a "good adoptive family" is abandoned.

Finally, the family assessment model presented in this volume is informed throughout by an ecological systems perspective. Such a perspective has relevance to the assessment process, not only in terms of the kinds of data gathered but also in terms of evaluation. Throughout the presentation of the assessment tools, their use in evaluation will be exemplified. In general, however, the family is seen as a transactional system, in constant interchange with its extended environment and developing intergenerationally through time.

Focus for understanding and planning is on the transactional relationships between people and environments, rather than on the essential character of the elements of these complex systems. The focus of work is to help prospective adoptive couples become experts on their family and their ecological environment, so that they may understand the implications of their interest in adoption and the possible outcomes of altering their family system by the addition of a new member.

However, before this shared evaluation process can begin between a social worker and any applicant, the participants must come together, clarify their roles and tasks in the process, and come to some sort of working agreement.

In Chapter 3, we turn to the beginning phase of work with adoptive applicants.

NOTES

1. Charles Loring Brace, The Dangerous Classes of New York. New York: Wynkoop and Hallenbeck, 1872, pp. 231-232.

2. H. Hart, "Placing Out Children in the West," Proceedings of the National Conference of Charities and Corrections, 1884, p. 143.

3. Quoted from 27th Annual Report of the Boston C.A.S., 1891, pp. 10-31 in Henry Thurston, The Dependent Child. New York: Columbia University Press, 1930.

4. Lesley, "Foundlings and Deserted Children," Proceedings of the National Conference of Charities and Corrections, 1884, p. 291.

5. Dorothy Hutchinson, In Quest of Foster Parents. New York: Columbia University Press, 1943, p. 52.

6. Ibid.

7. Hutchinson, op. cit., p. 12.

8. Hutchinson, op. cit., p. 62.

9. Hutchinson, op. cit., p. 26.

10. See Frieda M. Kuhlman and Helen P. Robinson, "Rorschach Tests As a Diagnostic Tool in Adoption Studies," Social Casework 32:1 (1950), pp. 15-22.

11. Henry Maas, "The Successful Adoptive Parent Applicant," Social Work 5:1 (January, 1960), pp. 14-20.

12. Alfred Kadushin, Child Welfare Services. New York: Macmillan, 1974, pp. 529-534.

13. Alfred Kadushin, "A Study of Adoptive Parents of Hard-to-Place Children," Social Casework 43:6 (May, 1962), pp. 227-234.

14. Kadushin, op. cit., pp. 227-228.

15. Kadushin, op. cit., p. 231.

16. Trudy Bradley, An Exploration of Caseworkers' Perceptions of Adoptive Applicants. New York: Child Welfare League of America, 1966.

17. Celia Bass, "Matchmaker-Matchmaker: Older Child Adoption Failures," Child Welfare LIV:7 (July, 1975), p. 506.

18. Ibid., p. 510.

19. New York City Department of Social Services, Policy Statement on Adoption, 1978. Unpublished document.

20. Ray L. Birdwhistell, "The American Family: Some Perspectives," Psychiatry 29 (1966), p. 212.

21. Frederick Duhl, "Intervention, Therapy, and Change," p. 400 in William Gray, Frederick Duhl, and Nicholas Rizzo (eds.), General Systems Theory and Psychiatry. Boston: Little, Brown, 1969.

Chapter 3

GETTING STARTED

Potential adoptive families find their way to adoption agencies by a variety of routes. Before the assessment process may begin, certain initial steps of engagement, contracting, and relationship development must take place.

ENGAGEMENT AND CONTRACTING

The potential adoptive parent or parents usually approach an adoption agency with anxiety and misconceptions, with information randomly gathered about adoptive procedures that is both accurate and inaccurate. They have heard about the agency; perhaps they have read publicity about the need for adoptive homes.

They are usually uncertain about the step they are contemplating, uncertain about what is to be expected of them, and most of all, concerned about what they envision as an evaluative process. The worker, on the other hand, approaches the encounter with very different perceptions and expectations.

The task of reaching a common understanding, of clarifying roles for worker and parent, of identifying shared goals, and specifying the steps to be taken to reach these goals is the process of engagement and beginning contracting. Many agencies begin the process with group meetings of adoptive parents. These meetings are generally educative sessions in which parents learn about the kinds of children that are available, and the questions and issues that should be considered in making a decision to adopt.

In one agency, this initial meeting is followed by a seminar where these issues are discussed in depth. This seminar was planned to also include persons who were themselves adopted and persons who released children for adoption.[1] This group educational experience develops a self selection process. The adoptive parents who choose to continue with their applications have a good understanding of what may lie ahead.

The Lutheran Social Service of Kansas and Oklahoma has made extensive use of parents who have adopted children as part of the helping team, both in groups and through family-to-family visits. These adoptive family volunteers participate in the early phases of education and engagement, and they continue to help through the total process including offering postadoptive services. The model at this agency includes a two-day meeting early in the application process that involves professional staff, adoptive parent volunteers, and prospective adoptive parents.[2]

Beginning the education and engagement process in group meetings is a useful procedure if well done. However, the danger in such meetings is that they may become purely informational sessions where agency representatives selectively "tell" prospective parents what these professionals feel they should know.

Straight informational meetings are probably less productive than no meeting at all. First, if people have strong misconceptions or anxieties about something, information given to the contrary tends to conceal rather than alter these views. Once people discover their ideas are different or even wrong, they are less likely to discuss them, but that does not mean they are relinquishing them.

A group session, or an individual one, should start with an opportunity for parents to express their confusions, concerns, and questions. Information should be given only after comments are heard and accepted. The advantage of the group, of course, is that many of the misconceptions and concerns will be shared by other group members. This sharing can increase openness and comfort in discussion.

The second potential problem with a purely informational session is that it tends to model an authoritarian rather than an egalitarian relationship. This kind of modeling belies and has more power than statements made by the staff to the contrary. The effectiveness of group meetings depends primarily on the degree to which the staff are willing to hear the concerns, engage the issues, and challenge the resistance presented by group members rather than seek the role of information giver that carries considerably less risk.

But whether the engagement process is initiated in a group or takes place in individual sessions, the tasks are the same. These tasks, which will be discussed separately, take place concurrently. They include moving toward congruence, establishing a working agreement, and developing mutual trust.

MOVING TOWARD CONGRUENCE

One process in developing a working relationship may be called moving toward congruence of expectations. This process has been explored as a part of role induction; for example, the process of inducting a person into the adoptive applicant role. Moving toward congruence of expectations means that two or more people move to the point where they each have the same understanding of their own and the other's role and behavior in the relationship they are developing and the shared tasks upon which they are embarking. A considerable amount of interpersonal difficulty and communication confusion may well arise from unexpressed incongruence of expectations.

Figure 3.1, developed by Brett Seabury,[3] illustrates the process of moving toward congruence. Clearly, for a relationship to "work," there has to be a reasonable amount of congruence or similarity between the two sets of diagonal squares. If this does not exist, the people involved tend to talk at cross purposes, feel tension, and often have a sense of distrust.

It is understandable that in the beginning phases of the relationship between adoptive parents and worker, there would be considerable incongruence. For example, at the beginning of the contact, the worker may expect to:

— help applicants make decision regarding adoption;

— help applicants understand as much as possible about adoption and about their own family in order to make good decision;

— help applicants consider possibility of adopting a child with special needs;

— have a series of interviews with the family to achieve the above purposes, if there are areas that need to be strengthened or altered in order to ready a family to take a particular child; and

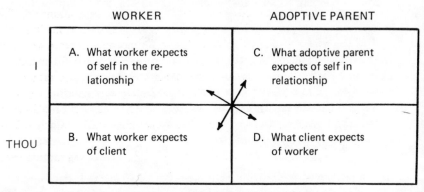

Figure 3.1 DEVELOPING RELATIONSHIP CONGRUENCE

— share thinking honestly with family.

The adoptive family, on the other hand, may see the worker's role quite differently.

— Worker will investigate, evaluate us, and decide whether or not we can have a child. The worker is looking for "perfect" families. If worker decides we are O.K., she or he will place a baby in our home.

— Worker is a professional and will not tell us what she or he thinks.

The incongruence here is obvious. The worker's first task is to try to help the parents alter their conception of the process and the worker's role. The worker will do this by exploring their perceptions and explaining his or her role.

The same kind of incongruence will probably exist between the worker's and the parents' conception of the parents' roles. The worker may define the parents' role as follows:

— the applicant must be ready to share a good deal about themselves to facilitate the process;

— the applicant should trust the worker and understand that the worker is there to help;

— the parent need not fear sharing problems or difficulties in the family as this will be perceived as honesty, openness, and healthy insight; and

— the parent should take an active, participatory role and not wait for the worker to take leadership in decision-making.

The adoptive applicants, however, may define their behavior in the situation quite differently.

— We must be very careful about what we say and attempt to anticipate what the worker wants to hear.

— We must "play it close to the chest" because if they learn anything negative we will not get a child.

— We are supposed to look like an "ideal" family.

Negotiation of this difference in understanding of the parents' role in the process, the importance of sharing, the parents' major responsibility for decision-making, and abandonment of the ideal family picture are among the most difficult parts of the engagement process.

ESTABLISHING A WORKING AGREEMENT

Developed concurrently with the move toward congruence is the contracting process. As clarity in role relationships grows out of moving toward congruence, contracting grows out of complementarity between the worker and the adoptive applicants. If the worker's purpose and the parents' purpose are not in conflict but, on the contrary, serve each other, they may join together to pursue their goals. Further, each has need of the other in reaching their objectives, which strengthens the complementarity.

The worker and parent come together because the worker is a part of an agency that has been sanctioned to place children for adoption and the parent wants a child. Out of this common purpose grows a "worker/parent agreement" or "contract," describing the steps to be taken to achieve the goal of placement and the tasks to be performed by the worker and the parents. The parents should have a very clear idea of what lies ahead. They should understand their responsibility in sharing and decision-making. They should know in advance about expected number of contacts, about legal aspects of adoption, and about postadoption requirements and services.

There is one area of seeming noncomplementarity between the worker/agency purpose and the parents' purpose and that may grow out of the worker's responsibility to the child. In a situation where the worker and agency feel that the potential adoptive parent is not ready to adopt or that the agency does not have a child whose needs could be met in their home, these judgements may fly in the face of the parents' wish for a child. Resolution may occur in one of two ways. First, the worker can pursue his or her role as a helper of the parents who are preparing to become adoptive parents. This is a new role for most adoption workers.

In most programs the tasks of the adoption worker were limited to evaluating homes, making placements, and offering limited postplacement services. An expanded view would suggest that the worker could become involved with the family in planning change that would ready them for adoption. Such plans could be directed at changes in the family's relationship with their ecological environment. For example, the worker may feel that the family does not have sufficient resources or a sufficiently viable social network to take on the complex and difficult task of adopting a needful child.

The worker may feel that the request for adoption may, in part, be an effort to solve an intrafamilial or intrapersonal problem. There may be tension in the marriage. There may be a painful unresolved loss. The potential adoptive mother may be seeking a solution to a lack of a sense of self worth or a feeling of emptiness in her life. These problems should not automatically rule out an adoptive family, but they should be addressed and resolved before a decision is made. This kind of family help may be available from the adoption worker, within the adoption agency, or through a referral by the adoption agency to another service provider. In cases where there is an unresolved disagreement between the agency and the parents as to the parents' readiness to adopt, the worker continues to act out of concern for the family. No family is served by having to experience the pain and the failure of a broken adoption. In these evaluations, however, it is essential that the worker be absolutely honest in sharing his or her thinking with the parents. This can be done without being destructive or hurtful as long as the explanation is highly specific and descriptive.

The importance of honesty in dealing with this issue cannot be overestimated. Much of the anger felt by parents who have been refused by agencies may well be connected with feelings of helplessness they experience because of their sense, often founded on fact, that the agency or worker is being secretive and is not giving them a clear and understandable explanation.

With an extended joint decision-making process and with the possibility of working with families to help them become ready to adopt, there would probably be very few situations in which worker and adoptive applicants differ as to the latter's readiness to adopt.

DEVELOPING MUTUAL TRUST

As the worker and adoptive applicants move toward congruence and fashion their working agreement, a relationship begins to develop. In fact, it is out of the clear, honest and open discussion of purpose, role, and tasks that a relationship of trust grows. The worker's identification with the adoptive parents' wish to have a child and his or her interest in helping the family obtain this goal strengthens the growing relationship. At this point, the stage is set for moving on into the assessment process.

NOTES

1. Graeme Gregory, "No Child Is Unadoptable," presented at the general meeting, Children's Welfare Association of Victoria, October, 1972. This article describes the model developed by Clayton Hagen, Lutheran Social Service, Minneapolis, Minnesota. Unpublished document.

2. Evelyn Middlestadt, "A Model for Professional-Adoptive Parent Team Work in Adoption of Older Children," 1975, mimeo.

3. Brett A. Seabury and Jay R. Ballew, Reuniting Families: Working with the Families of Children in Foster Care, unpublished manuscript.

Chapter 4

AN ECOLOGICAL FRAMEWORK FOR ASSESSMENT

Ecology has, in recent years, occupied more and more of the nation's attention and concern. We have become increasingly aware of the complex and often fragile balance that exists in nature. We have learned that all living things are dependent on each other for survival. We have learned that the unforeseen consequences of progress have too often disrupted these important relationships, and we now know that even the most well-intentioned intervention may lead to further destruction.

The science of ecology studies the sensitive balance that exists between living things and their environments, and the ways in which this mutuality may be enhanced and maintained. Social workers recently have attempted to use the ecological metaphor to provide a new way of thinking about and understanding what has always been the central focus of social work, "person-in-situation." This stance may be most useful in the assessment process in adoption practice.

When we adopt this view, however, we find we must deal with an extremely complex ecological system. A consideration of the human environment does not include just concern for the quality of air, water, food, spacial arrangements, and other aspects of the physical environment. Over the centuries, human beings have erected elaborate social, economic, and political structures that they must sustain and through which their needs are met. People must maintain an adaptive mutuality with the intricate human systems that they require for growth and self realization, and with the elaborate social environment that they have constructed.

ASSESSING THE FAMILY ECOLOGY

Utilizing an ecological model for assessment in social work leads us to focus on the complex ecological system that includes the family and the total environment, and the transactional relationships between that family and the environment. This view focuses on the sources of nurturance, stimulation, and support that must be available from both the intimate and the extended social environment to make growth and survival possible.

Adopting an ecological systems perspective extends the unit of attention, and leads one to a mass of complex interrelated data. As a result, the EcoMap was devised as an interviewing and assessment tool that could capture and organize this complexity.

The EcoMap is constructed with the potential adoptive family. Its use helps the family consider the quality of their life space. An ecological view not only recognizes that stress and conflict are always a part of the world of any living system, but also that some sort of balance must be achieved between stress and support, between demands and resources, for a system to survive and grow. The EcoMap leads a family to assess whether they have an excess of resources, whether they are already stressed, or without sufficient support. This kind of analysis helps the potential adoptive parent wonder what impact a child, with all his or her needs, demands and requirements, may have on the balance currently being maintained in the family's ecological system.

Beginning with the EcoMap tends to help the adoptive applicant feel comfortable and undefensive. The focus is on the life space, and the kind of data requested is concrete and not extremely personal. The map also, in a very dramatic way, introduces the family to a systems orientation and to the fact that it is not they as individuals that are being evaluated, but rather that a joint effort is being made to understand a total ecological system.

If there are any children in the potential adoptive family, it is often helpful to involve them at this point in the assessment process—children enjoy ecomapping. The map makes sense to them and gives them an opportunity to actively participate through telling about the important elements in their life space. It also enables them to consider how their world might change should a new brother or sister enter their home.

INSTRUCTIONS FOR ECOMAPPING

An EcoMap may be done with an empty piece of paper, or it may be constructed by completing a blank EcoMap similar to the one that follows

(Figure 4.1). Each procedure has certain advantages. Starting without any structure may lead to somewhat more flexibility. Use of the structured map, however, is a time-saver and also quickly suggests to those participating what the procedure is all about. It may be easier to learn ecomapping by following the structured map.

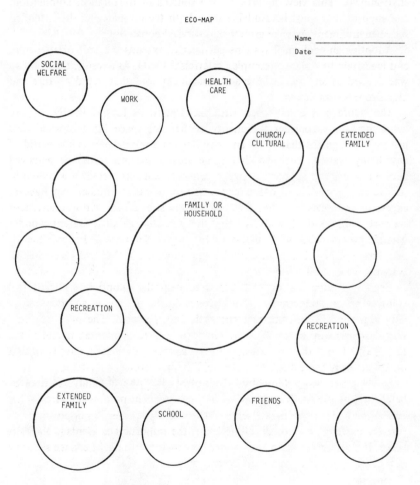

Figure 4.1 ECOMAP

Within the large circle in the middle of the EcoMap, chart the members of the household. This is done as follows: A woman is indicated by a circle: ○ ; a man, by a square: □ . A married couple is portrayed as follows:

It is often useful to add their names and ages. Perhaps, Bill and Ann have two sons, also living in the home.

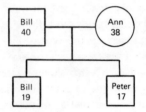

Ann's mother came to live with them after her father died.

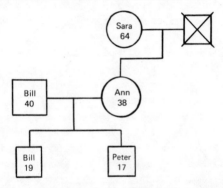

This, then, is a picture of the household. The usefulness of pictures is already demonstrated when one considers the number of words it would take to communicate the facts represented in the EcoMap.

A single parent, divorced, mother of one son and living with her parents would be pictured as follows:

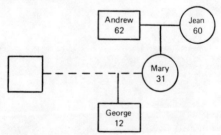

The mapping of more complex family systems will be demonstrated in the discussion of genograms that follows in Chapter 5.

Having pictured the household within the large circle in the middle of the EcoMap, the next step is to begin to draw in the connections between the family and the different parts of the ecological environment. Some of the most common systems in the lives of most families, such as work, extended family, recreation, health care, school, and so on, have been labelled in the blank map. Other circles have been left undesignated so that the map is sufficiently flexible to be individualized for different families.

Connections between the family and the various systems are indicated by drawing lines between the family and those systems. The nature of the connection may be expressed by the type of line drawn. A solid or thick line indicates an important or strong connection. A broken line indicates a tenuous connection. A hatched line shows a stressful or conflicted relationship. It is also very useful to indicate the direction of the flow of resources, energy, or interest by drawing arrows along the connecting lines.

In testing out the EcoMap, we have found that the use of the three kinds of lines for conflicted, strong, and tenuous relationships is an efficient shorthand when the worker uses the ecomapping procedure as an analytic tool without the family's direct participation. When using the map as an interviewing tool, however, this type of line code has often been felt to be too constraining. Workers prefer to ask applicants to describe the nature of the connection and then qualify that connection by writing a descriptive word or two along the connecting line.

Some of the connections may be drawn to the family or household as a whole when they are intended to portray the total group's relationship with some system in the environment. Other connections may be drawn between a particular individual and an outside system when that person is the only one involved, or different family members are involved with an outside system in different ways. This differentiation enables the map to highlight contrasts in the way various family members are connected with the world.

It is easy to learn to do the EcoMap, and it is important to become comfortable with it before using the EcoMap with adoptive applicants. A simple way to learn is to do one's own EcoMap. It is also useful to practice with a friend or two.

THE ECOMAP IN USE WITH POTENTIAL ADOPTIVE PARENTS

The primary use of the EcoMap is as an interviewing and assessment tool, to be used as a springboard for discussion and as a visual aid around which to integrate the details of the adoptive family's relationship with the ecological environment. Not only is the ecomapping session a good time to include any children in the family, but also other important people in the life space; for example, a grandparent who lives in the home or nearby.

The process of mapping invites active participation. After all, it is the family's map, and no one knows their world as they do. The task of mapping is shared, and the participatory relationship is expressed in action as worker

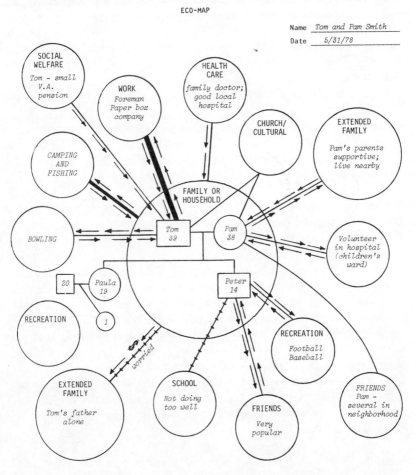

Figure 4.2 ECOMAP—TOM AND PAM SMITH

and family tend to move closer together and end shoulder-to-shoulder, absorbed in the joint project.

The kinds of material and relationships that may emerge from work on the mapping process are varied, and may range from a rather simple and straight-forward assessment of the resources available to a complex analysis of the different ways different family members are relating to the world.

The map in Figure 4.2 pictures a family with many resources and interests. They have rewarding social connections with friends and community, and

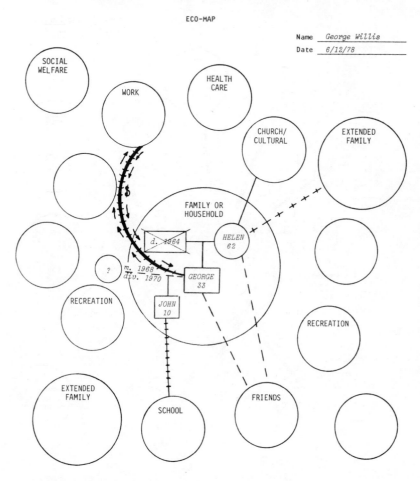

ECO-MAP

Name _George Willis_
Date _6/12/78_

Fill in connections where they exist.
Indicate nature of connections with a descriptive word or by drawing different kinds of lines; ———— for strong, ------- for tenuous, ++++ for stressful.
Draw arrows along lines to signify flow of energy, resources, etc. → → →
Identify significant people and fill in empty circles as needed.

Figure 4.3 ECOMAP—GEORGE WILLIS

have relationships of mutual aid with extended family members. There is stress, of course, as there is in any family. For example, Tom and Pam are concerned about Tom's recently widowed and aging father, and Tom's job, although paying well, makes extremely heavy demands on his time and energy.

The marital pair enjoy some activities together but also have separate interests. In terms of the two children in the family, Paula left the parental home for an early marriage, and the adoptive applicants are very young

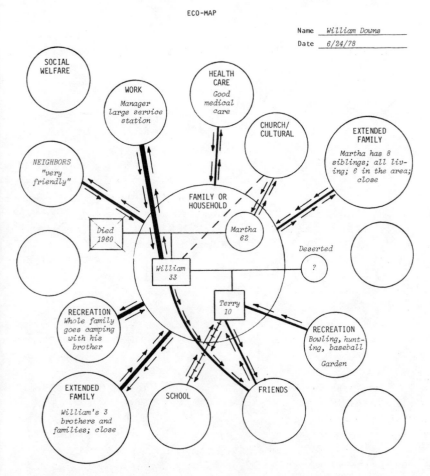

Figure 4.4 ECOMAP—WILLIAM DOWNS

grandparents. There appears to be some stress around Peter's school life, although he has many friends and is active in sports.

Two quite different maps of two single parent families of similar structure follow. In the map of George's world shown in Figure 4.3, it is apparent that he and his son are isolated socially and have few sources of support and stimulation. In fact, George, his son, and his mother who participated together in the mapping session, give evidence of being a rather closed system. Is George's interest in adopting a six to nine-year-old boy an effort to deal with the family's loneliness and his wish to "give" his son a sibling to heal his aloneness? What potential burden would this imply for a child coming into this home?

William Downs' map in Figure 4.4 portrays a family of similar demographic characteristics, including occupation, income, and structure. However, in this map we see an open system with a variety of lively connections with the life space. An examination of the ecological system gives evidence of many sources of support and stimulation, opportunities for self-actualization and development. The system looks rich enough in human resources to meet the needs of another young person coming into the situation.

In the Figure 4.3 map, as George, Helen, John, and the worker study it together, the visual image of isolation and social impoverishment may be shared. The worker may comment, "This looks like a very lonely family to me." Such an observation may lead to a further exploration of the family's pattern of excluding contact and drawing away from the world. Out of this kind of discussion may come a recognition on the family's part of some of this loneliness, and of the wish to adopt as a solution to the family's difficulties in developing and maintaining social connections.

Not only does the EcoMap lead to an assessment of the family's life situation but, in this case, it could also lead to a decision and a plan. A child cannot heal a family's pain. The task that lies ahead for George and his family is to prepare for adoption by opening up the boundaries of their isolated family and building connections with the world. This very process may diminish the wish for a child and the request may be withdrawn. On the other hand, should George's interest in adoption persist, the worker and George may continue to work together toward the achievement of the goal.

AN ECOMAPPING INTERVIEW

The following transcription of an ecomapping interview with a couple considering the adoption of an older child demonstrates the richness of the process and the complexity of the system. The interview is followed by Figure 4.5, the EcoMap that was produced in the session, and by a discussion of the interview and the understanding of the family system in its life space that grew out of this discussion.

This interview took place between David and Marge Singer and the adoption worker, Bill Dalton. The couple had been seen together with three other couples in an application group, had a good understanding of the agency, the kinds of children that were generally available for adoption, and the adoption procedure. Following the initial introduction to the process, they had decided to continue exploring with the staff their interest in adopting a boy of around eight or nine years of age.

This was the first interview alone with the couple. The worker used the ecomapping procedure as an interviewing tool. The portion of the interview that was devoted to ecomapping is included. All names are fictitious. The interview opened with some discussion of the group meeting. Marge had a couple of questions that had occurred to her since the meeting, and these were discussed.

Bill: What I'd like to do today is for us to begin to get a better understanding of the world your family lives in—sort of begin to see your family members in their daily life—in their everyday world.

Marge: Uh, huh.

Bill: (showing the couple an empty EcoMap) This is a map that we often use here to begin to get a picture of the family in its world. We call it an EcoMap, you know, short for "ecological." I thought we could fill one of these out together today.

Marge: O.K. with me.

David: Me, too.

Bill: All we'll do is identify the various people, activities, and things that are a part of your family's life, and draw lines between the family member and that part of their world to show the connection.

David: I don't really see. . . .

Bill: Maybe if we get started, you'll see how it goes. Let's start with inside the big circle—who's in the household? There's you, David. We'll put a square (I don't know why men are shown by squares but they always are!) How old are you?

David: I'm 46.

Bill: And here you are, Marge. How old are you?

Marge: I'm 45.

Bill: O.K. Now, what about the names and ages of your kids?

Marge: Peter's the oldest—he's 16. Then Matthew, 14, and the baby, Daryl, we call him Dee, he's seven. There's a thing about "Ds" in the family.

Bill: What do you mean?

Marge: Well, there's Dee and David, and David's father was Daniel, and his grandfather was Donald.

David: Yep, that's right.

Bill: That is a lot of Ds! Anyone else in the household?

Marge: There's Grover, the dog.

Bill: That's a wonderful name for a dog. We'll stick him in.

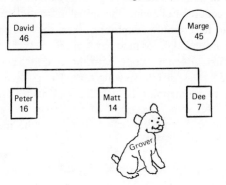

Bill: Now, shall we start with work? This is the work circle here.

Marge: Yes, that seems like a good place. It sure occupies a big part of the family's time.

Bill: What do you mean?

Marge and David both told about their jobs with considerable animation. David is a computer operator in a power company. Marge is deeply involved in her position as a special education teacher. Quite early, with some bantering back and forth, it becomes obvious that David is a "loner" whereas Marge is very involved and active socially.

They move on to a discussion of housework that Marge has always hated and her insistence that the boys share the household tasks.

David: (Laughing) It's this woman's lib thing. She thinks the boys should be able to do all that.

Marge: Absolutely! I think it's important for them to be able to take care of themselves, not to always have to depend on a woman. And, they're really getting pretty good. Dee cleaned the bathroom last night when I was out at a meeting. He really did a neat job! This housework thing has always been a bug-a-boo for me. I was climbing the walls after Peter and Matthew were born. They were 20 months apart, and David was under a lot of pressure at work. I was feeling pretty overwhelmed.

Bill: But what about after Dee? Was it the same then?

Marge: No, it was different then. I went back to school when Matt was
         three. In fact, I started part-time before that. It really saved my life.
         But that's why the gap. I feel badly about that.
Bill: The gap?
Marge: Yes. The gap between Matt and Dee—the seven years. I was getting
         my career organized. We had wanted four children but just didn't
         have the one we should have had between Matt and Dee. In some
         ways it's made Dee like an only child.
Bill: So that's one of the reasons you've been thinking about adoption?
David: Yeah, Marge wants to fill in the gap!
Marge: Dee's alone too much. He always has been. It worries me. I never
         wanted an only child, not that he is exactly, but I do feel badly
         about that gap.
Bill: (Turning to the EcoMap) What about the kids? What kinds of
         activities are they involved in?

   The parents report in detail about each of the boys' activities, and the
information is added to the map. Peter is described as an athelete, an
outdoorsman, and a hard worker at his part-time job. Matt is identified with
Marge as a "social butterfly" and a leader in school; and Dee is seen as a loner
interested in science like his father.
   The parents then tell about their own activities. David's main interest is in
his garden, but Marge is involved in many activities. "What makes Marge
run?" David cracks.

Marge: He means I'm going all the time, and he's right. What with my job,
         which I love, and friends, and community work; but, I always or
         almost always get home the same time as the kids do from school.
         But I do a lot in the evening, too. I've been active in politics, and
         I've been a volunteer at the woman's crisis center. It's just the way I
         am.
Bill: What about your neighborhood?
Marge: I guess we made a mistake on that. When we bought the house—I
         don't know, I told you it's a big old house. The room is wonderful,
         but it's been an awful burden financially. Neither of us are handy
         and people who aren't handy shouldn't have an old house. The
         repair bills have been killing us.
David: He asked about the neighborhood.
Marge: Oh, I was getting to that. The other trouble is the neighborhood.
         Most of the people are older. There are very few kids around. We

really haven't had too much in common with our neighbors. I've mainly made friends through work, politics, and the crisis center.

David: In a way, I like it that way. I wouldn't want to be in one of those neighborhoods where people are always in and out of your house.

Bill: What about friends?

Marge: Well, we have different kinds of friends, in a way. There are mainly two couples from our old neighborhood—when we first came here. Dave likes the husbands, and I like the wives. We don't see an awful lot of them, but if we ever needed anything, all we's have to do is say so and they'd be here. I wish we did see more of them. And then there's my friends—the people I've gotten to know through work and my activities—mainly women. I've tried to turn it into a couple thing but it's hard. Two wives throw the two husbands together, but it just doesn't work.

David: It works out O.K., though. Marge has more time and likes to socialize more. I don't mind if she has her own social life. So she does her thing. . . .

Marge: And you do yours.

Bill: Here are the extended family circles. How about your families?

David and Marge report that both their families are far away and that there is not as much contact as they would like. David's mother died the previous year, leaving his stepfather alone, at eighty. David also has a sister several years his senior who, Marge reports with anger, has never visited despite their many efforts to have more contact.

Marge's family is described as living far away but "close." She has a mother still living and two brothers. Marge reports that she dreams of someday moving to New Hampshire to be near her brothers.

Bill: (Picking up on the sadness in Marge's voice) As I look at your map, I can see your lives are very full and busy, but I also get a certain sense of social isolation. I don't know. What do you think?

David: I wouldn't call it isolation. We're not real sociable—at least Dee's not and I'm not. But it doesn't seem isolated.

Marge: I think it is, really. Look at the map. There are no lines between you and anything but work and gardening.

David: And family. I mean you and the kids. Isn't that enough?

Bill: The issue is really what works for you and for your family, and how would it work to bring a new child into the home?

Marge: I think it works O.K. for us. I wish David were more . . . involved with people. I guess that's what was going on early in our marriage after Peter and Matt were born. I quit work when I was pregnant with Peter and boy, did the walls close in! That was a rugged time. Not that I wasn't thrilled with the boys. But speaking of isolation— David was working all the time; money was really tight, and we couldn't afford sitters very much. That was a really low point! That's why I went back to school and to work. I'm not cut out to be home all the time. I've worked or gone to school ever since, except for the six months leave when Dee was born. You don't have to be a 100 percent homebody to adopt a child, do you?

Bill: No. Families work out all kinds of ways of living. There's no one right way to be a parent.

Marge: Yes, that's what they said in the group meeting. We wouldn't have continued looking into this otherwise, I guess.

Bill: As we go along, we do want to figure out together what it would do to your EcoMap to put another child into the family. What kinds of changes and shifts might take place?

David: I can see that.

Returning to the map, Bill asks about cultural interests and religion. David and Marge report on the family's cultural connections including David's interest in music, and their tenuous connection with religion although they readily volunteered that they would support an adopted child's connection with religion.

They then moved on to a discussion of health. David emerges as excessively concerned about his health and Marge as rather neglectful of health issues, particularly about her own health. Out of the discussion about health, comes the information that David relies on intellectual mastery in any area where he feels anxious or must make a decision. Marge reports that he has been reading up on adoption for months.

David: Whenever I'm faced with any kind of problem or decision, I want all the facts. With my scientific approach and her intuition, I guess we do O.K.

Bill: Well, is there anything you want to add to the map? Can you think of anything we've left out?

David: You know, it's really interesting when you look at the whole picture. I don't think I even saw us quite like this before.

Bill: What do you see?

David: Well, I can see how different Marge and I are—in the way we relate to the world. She's got a whole lot of lines going, and I don't.

Marge: Yes, and look. Dee's the same way, like David. I don't want him to grow up like that—I mean a loner.

David: You mean you don't want him to be like me?

Marge: In a lot of ways, yes, but in some ways, no.

David: Well, I don't think bringing a brother into the family for him to play with is going to make him into a different kind of kid—make him social.

Marge: Yes, I guess you're right. Maybe that is what I'm trying to do.

Bill: One of the things you have to remember when you think about all this is that most of the children we have, have had a lot of hurt, a lot of pain, and a lot of needs. I don't know that it's going to work for you to be thinking, for instance, about what a child can do for Dee.

Marge: Yes, you're right. I know better than that. But the three boys—it's always the two older ones and then Dee is odd man out. He should have had that other brother.

David: You mean that one you didn't have when you went back to work.

Marge: Yes, I seem to feel I have to make it up to him. It's silly, I mean, or me to feel this way.

Bill: Feelings aren't silly. They're important and our job, together, is to try to understand them and what they have to do with this adoption decision. You know, I've been thinking. This feeling about wanting the fourth child. It's funny. It's almost the third child to fill the gap. That would make Dee the fourth, if you see what I mean.

David: Yes, I get it.

Bill: Well, anyway, this also might have something to do with the families you grew up in too. Perhaps next time we get together we can talk about that. We can do a genogram. That's a map, like the EcoMap— but it's a map of the family.

David: Fine.

Marge: My Lord! I just thought of something. My mother lost a child—I mean I think it was full term, stillborn—a boy when I was about 6. Wow!

Bill: That might have something to do with all this. We'll have to do the genograms and think together about these things.

Marge: That blows my mind! Maybe that's the third child!

David: Oh, Marge, now don't get carried away.

Bill: Well, it's certainly something to think about.

After making arrangements for the next meeting together, Marge and David left.

ECO-MAP

Name ___Singer___

Date ___6/5/78___

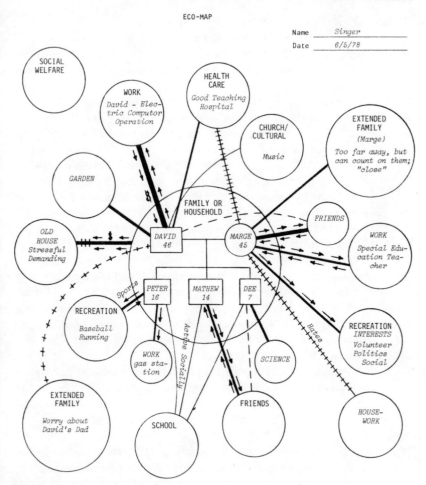

Fill in connections where they exist.
Indicate nature of connections with a descriptive work or by drawing different kinds of
  lines; ———— for strong, ------ for tenuous, +++++ for stressful.
Draw arrows along lines to signify flow of energy, resources, etc. → → →
Identify significant people and fill in empty circles as needed.

Figure 4.5 ECOMAP–SINGER FAMILY

LOOKING AT THE INTERVIEW

In thinking about the interview, Bill had the following impressions: This couple had been very open, sharing and had really involved themselves in the process. They had begun to learn more about their family in ways that would lead them closer to making a good decision. David's wish to study and

understand and Marge's "psychological mindedness" made them active participants in this assessment task.

On the basis of the session, Bill had some hypotheses about the family, to
be shared with them and explored further. Marge was taking the lead in the
session. The interest in adoption may come more strongly from her than from
David. Part of this, however, may be a result of Marge's function in the family
as the "communicator" and as the one who deals with interpersonal tasks.
Marge speaks a lot for David, so it's going to be harder to find out where
David is on this.

In terms of the EcoMap, there seems to be a lot of demands and minimum
supportive resources. The couple, after early struggles around this, has been
able to allow each other to develop the kinds of relationships with the world
that satisfy them. However, there appears to be some residual tension about
this, shown in David's defensiveness and a theme expressed by Marge of
longing for closeness.

The theme of loneliness frequently emerges. Marge has become aware in
the course of the session, that part of her motive for wanting to adopt may be
to make up to Dee for his "odd man out" status, and for her guilt about
seeking her own interests rather than having that third child. Further, David
picked up, and very astutely pointed out, that Marge may want to bring
another child into the home to change Dee, so he won't be like his Dad—a
loner.

Marge is dealing with her needs by a lot of involvement in the outside
world, and is a little apologetic about the amount of her energy that is going
outward. Another needful and demanding child might well force Marge to
pull in, to focus more of her energy in the home and family. Would she begin
to experience this as "the walls closing in?"

As far as other aspects of the EcoMap, basic essentials were available—for
income, housing, transportation, schools, activities. On the health issue, the
location of a teaching hospital in their community is a particularly valuable
resource if we come to consider placement of a child with a health problem
that needs special facilities.

The discovery by Marge, at the end of the interview, of the possible
connection of the adoption request with the lost brother will be explored.
This leads the family very naturally to begin to work on the genogram.

Chapter 5

ASSESSMENT IN TIME: THE GENOGRAM

We have looked at the family as it is immersed in its environment and as it interacts with the various systems in the life space. The family not only exists in space, but it has also developed through time. The emphasis on the use of family history in understanding the current life of the individual and the family grows from the conviction that the main source of each person's sense of self and personal identity is to be found in the saga of his or her family.

The starting point of this approach is an assumption that all people are deeply immersed in their family systems. It affects people's perceptions of who they are, how they think and communicate, and how they see themselves and others. It influences what they choose to do and be, whom they choose to be with and to love and marry, and how they choose to structure their new family.

THE INTERGENERATIONAL FAMILY HISTORY

The exploration of intergenerational family history leads to an enhanced understanding of the dynamics of the current family and may help clarify the meaning of the wish to adopt. It may lead to an understanding of why a couple feels their family is incomplete or why adoption is sought as a way to build a family. It may be used to surface the expectations and role assignments of a child who steps into a particular spot in the family tree.

The genogram is a useful way of gathering and organizing family history. It is a family tree or a map of three or more generations of a family that records genealogical relationships, major family events, occupations, losses, family migrations and dispersal, identifications and role assignments, and information about alignment and communication patterns.

Drawing a genogram with adoptive applicants increases understanding of their family system and moves them closer to making an informed decision about adoption. It also often serves to get them in touch with the power and importance of their roots. This may lead the adoptive applicants to an appreciation of the meaning of biological family roots to a child they may bring into their home.

INSTRUCTIONS FOR DRAWING A GENOGRAM

It is best to approach drawing a genogram with a large piece of paper. It is important that the genogram is uncrowded and clear so visual examination is possible. Plain white pads, the size of desk blotters, with cardboard backing, available in office supply stores, are useful and convenient for this task.

The skeleton of the genogram tends to follow the conventions of genetic and genealogical charts. As in the EcoMap, male is indicated by a square: □ ; a female, by a circle: ○ ; and if the sex of a person is unknown, by a triangle: △ . The triangle tends to be used when a person says, "I think there were seven children in my grandfather's family, but I have no idea whether they were males or females," or, "My mother lost a full term child five years before I was born, but I don't know what sex it was."

A marital pair is indicated by □——○, and it is useful to add the marriage date, □—M. 6/2/54—○ . Offspring are shown as follows:

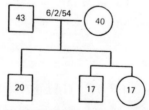

They are generally lined up according to age starting with the oldest on the left. The above family has an older son followed by a set of twins. A divorce is generally portrayed by a dotted line, and again, it is useful to include dates.

A family member no longer living is generally shown by ⊠ d. 1967. Thus, a complex, but not untypical, reconstituted family may be drawn as follows:

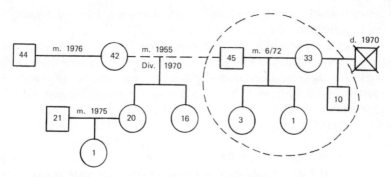

It is useful to draw a dotted line around the family members who compose the household. Incidentally, such a family chart enables the worker to quickly grasp "who's who" in complicated reconstituted families.

With these basic building blocks expanded horizonatally to depict the contemporary generation of siblings and cousins and vertically to chart the generations through time, it is possible to chart any family, given sufficient paper, patience, and information. As one charts the relationship structure of the family, it is also important to fill this out with the rich and varied data that portray the saga of the particular family.

SOME TIPS ABOUT THE GENOGRAM

Given names, both first and middle, identify family members, indicate naming patterns, and surface identifications. In constructing a genogram with a prospective adoptive couple, parents of three biological daughters, it emerged that the father carried the same name as his father, grandfather, and great grandfather. He spoke of this connection with nostalgic pride. This led him to tell about his heroic great grandfather who had been a lumberjack in northern Michigan.

He reminisced about the rugged hunting and fishing trips his grandfather, his father, and he had taken when he was a boy. What became apparent was the deep longing this man had for a son, a longing he was now hoping to satisfy through adoption. Also apparent was the heavy burden of expectation and the predetermined identity that was ready to fall upon the child's shoulders. What if the boy were little, skinny, afraid of animals, and hated the out-of-doors?

In connection with naming patterns in the family, it is very useful at this point to ask the adoptive parents if they have any thoughts about their potential adopted child's name. Who is the potential namesake? These questions help worker and parent to think together about how the child is already being identified.

In the case of an older child, the issue of changing the given name raises attitudes about the child's biological identity and the parents' ability to tolerate the fact that the child had a life, connections, and an established sense of self that predates his or her joining the family. As one adoptive couple said when they decided not to change their adopted baby's name, "It's a lovely name and besides, it's something her mother could give her, and we didn't want to take it away."

Dates of birth and dates of death record when members joined the family, longevity, and family losses. Birth dates indicate the age of family members when important events occurred. In a sense, birth, marriage, and death dates mark the movement of the family through time. Birth dates also identify each individual's place in the sibship. This is particularly important in considering the possible images applicants have of families and any strong feelings they have about building a family in a certain way.

The importance of birth information is highlighted in the EcoMap interview with the Singer family reported in Chapter 4. Marge kept referring to "filling the gap" in discussing her interest in adopting a boy of eight or nine years of age. What is apparent on one level is that Marge feels guilty about Dee's almost "only child status." She became involved in her own career. After a seven year "gap," she gave birth to Dee whom she sees as isolated and a "loner" like his father. This worries her. A look at the family's genogram surfaces other identifications and possible meanings implicit in the request for a child.

Singer's Genogram

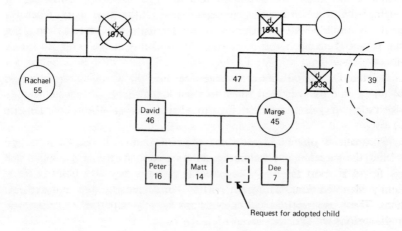

Request for adopted child

Marge's sibship is almost the same as the arrangement of her children. She and her older brother are close just as are Peter and Matt. She is obviously identified with Matt, who occupies the same place in the family and whom she describes the same way she describes herself. The stillborn brother who was born when she was four was located in the same place as would be the child she now wants to fit into her family.

A second level of understanding may indicate that adopting a son to "fill the gap" is also related to the unresolved loss of the third child in her family of origin. This is further confirmed by the identification of Dee with her younger brother to whom she feels less close than her older brother and who appears, like Dee, to be "odd man out" in that set of siblings.

Dee is also linked with his father's role in his family of origin. His father also was a much younger boy who was alone a good deal and felt isolated within his family.

Place of birth and current place of residence mark the movement of the family through space. Such information charts the family's patterns of dispersal, surfacing major immigrations or migrations, and brings attention to periods of loss, change, and upheaval. On the other hand, such information may point to the fact that generations of a family have stayed within a fairly small geographical radius.

Picturing the family's movement through space may communicate a good deal about family boundaries and norms concerning mobility. Is this a family that "holds on" or "lets go"? Locating family members in space begins to tap the extent to which the family continues to be intimately connected with extended family members. Is the extended family available and interested? What is their attitude toward the applicants' wish to adopt?

One white family that had expressed an interest in adopting a child of mixed racial heritage was discovered to be quite distant from their families of origin, both of which lived in the same county in the rural south. When the worker inquired about the extended family's reaction to their adoption plans, the potential adoptive couple assured the worker that the extended family did not know about this nor did they plan to tell them until the adoption was completed. On examination it became clear that the extended family would be angry and disapprove. It began to seem that at least part of the couple's motivation was related to their effort to rebel and separate from their families of origin.

Occupations of family members acquaint one with the interests and talents, the successes and failures, and the varied socioeconomic statuses that are found in most families. Occupational patterns may also point to intra-family identifications, and often portray family prescriptions and expectations. These prescriptions and expectations are very important to understand in discussions with families about adoption.

For example, if family occupations cover a wide range of blue and white collar positions and if some of the admired and valued members are in blue collar occupations, it may well indicate that a family can tolerate differences in interests and in educational level or achievement. This kind of acceptance of difference would, in all likelihood, be extended to the adopted child.

On the other hand, if everyone in the family has been college-bound except for Uncle Harry who works in road construction and is considered the family failure, a natural question arises: How would this family feel about a child of below average intellectual potential or with different occupational preferences than those expected in the family?

Finally, facts about family members' health and causes of death provide an overall family health history and also may say a good deal about the way a family views health, illness, and handicaps. Many of the children awaiting adoption are children with a range of physical and/or mental handicaps. Attaining the health history on the genogram may point to resources the family may have in making a home for a handicapped child.

For example, one family had an extended history of congenital deafness although no one in the immediate family had a hearing loss. The beloved grandmother had been deaf since girlhood, the two uncles were also deaf, as were several cousins. The deaf family members had led full and successful lives. This family was very comfortable considering a child with a severe hearing loss. The family had always taken deafness in its stride and felt a strong sense of identification with a child with impaired hearing.

The presence of a particular disability in a family may, however, have the opposite effect. The questions to be asked revolve around the attitude of the family toward the handicap and the ability of the family and the handicapped person to appropriately adapt and master the tasks involved in dealing with the disability. The same problem will be defined in one family as a major tragedy and in another as a challenge.

Attitudes toward health and disability are highly individual and are often related to the family's multigenerational experience. A discussion with the family about the health history leads quite naturally to a discussion of how the family might feel about and respond to a handicapped child.

The demographic data may take the adoption worker a long way toward understanding the family system. However, gathering associations about family members can add to the richness of the portrayal. One can ask, "What word or two, or what picture comes to mind when you think about this person?" These associations tend to tap another level of information about the family as the myths, role assignments, or characterizations of family members come to their minds. It is hard to predict whether the responses to these open-ended questions will be relevant to decision-making around adoption. In a sense, if you don't ask, you'll never know.

The most important and valuable thing about constructing the genogram is that it is an orderly way of getting family history and organizing that history so the worker and the adoptive family can look at it together. Drawing the genogram makes sure that the questions are asked, and if there are family patterns, myths, losses, illnesses that are important in considering the issue of adoption, they will not be inadvertently passed over.

HOW TO ANALYZE A GENOGRAM

Just as the adoptive applicant and the worker study the EcoMap together, so do they study the genogram to enhance their understanding of the family system and the wish to adopt. Sometimes the connections and patterns are obvious. For example, a black woman, mother of a ten-year-old daughter, wanted to adopt a second child, another girl. She was touched by the agency's publicity about the many black children in need of families. The woman approached the agency with the convinction that she and her daughter, with the support of her extended family, could offer a good home to a child.

She commented that many of her friends had expressed doubts and concerns saying, "Aren't you worried about the kind of child you might get? About getting into a real mess?" On the contrary. The woman approached adoption with considerable optimism. On constructing the genogram, she was reminded that her mother was adopted at the age of three following the death of her mother's biological mother. This had worked out very well and the applicant remembered her grandmother, her mother's adoptive mother, with great warmth.

The reasons for both her optimistic attitude and for her responsiveness to the agency's description of little girls without families became clearer. Interestingly enough, the applicant's mother had also maintained contact with some of her biological relatives while growing up and is still in touch with an old aunt, the sister of her biological mother.

A GENOGRAM INTERVIEW

The following report of an interview in which a genogram was used as an interviewing tool may serve to demonstrate how the genogram may be used and how it is charted. Finally, the genogram will be analyzed in an attempt to demonstrate how this simulation may be used to discover a great deal about a family system that has considerable relevance to the possibility of adoption.

The interview took place between Frank and Mary Scott and the adoption worker, Janet Landon. A couple in their early thirties, the Scotts approached the agency with an interest in adopting a boy. Their call was precipitated by a newspaper campaign that had been launched in their community, describing the need for black adoptive homes and the growing number of black children, particularly boys, who were growing up in "temporary foster care" because there were no adoptive homes available.

The Scotts had been thinking about adoption for some time. They had two daughters, seven and ten. Mary, following two very difficult deliveries, had been strongly advised not to have another child. The following is a transcription of a portion of the second interview Janet Landon, the worker, had with the couple.

Following their initial call, the Scotts had met with a group of adoptive applicants for a group intake session and then met with Janet for an ecomapping session. The EcoMap had pictured the family as actively involved in their environment. Frank worked as a foreman in a large manufacturing concern.

Mary, who had a degree in music education, augmented their income by giving piano lessons and serving as the assistant organist at church. Frank was interested in outdoor activities, particularly fishing. Both girls were involved with friends and activities. Lynn, the younger daughter, was not doing too well in school which gave her mother some concern. The family maintained close contact with both extended families, although they agreed that Frank's mother tended to be overinvolved at times.

After some greetings, the first few minutes of the meeting were devoted to a discussion of the EcoMap and certain new perspectives they had gained about the family's relationship with its life space.

Janet: Today, I'd like us to work on another map. It's called a genogram. It's a picture of your family—three generations or so. It's like a family tree, but it tells more about the people in the family.

Frank: Three generations! Wow—what's the point of all of that?

Janet: Well, a lot of people feel that families don't start the day two people get married, but that they grow and develop over the generations. One way to understand a family better is to map its development. Maybe the families that you two grew up in have a lot to do with the way your present family has developed.

Mary: Yes, I see what you mean. Sort of like *Roots.*

Janet: Yes, but not quite so far back. Would you like to do a genogram?

Frank: Sure, I'm game.

Janet: O.K., Frank. Let's start with you. When were you born?

Frank: May 20, 1943.

Janet: And where was that?

Frank: I was born in Detroit. No, I was *born* in Texas. My father was in the service, and my mother traveled around with him for a while. Right after I was born, she came back to Detroit to stay with her folks, and my father went overseas.

Janet: Were you the oldest?

Frank: Yes. In fact, I was the only child of that marriage. My parents split up right after the war—1945—and my mother remarried. They had two children—a boy and a girl.

Janet: So, you were raised by your mother and step-father?

Frank: Not really. I really stayed with my grandparents, until my grandmother died when I was a teenager. My mother lived in Detroit, but I had been with my grandparents so long I was six when my mother remarried, and my grandparents were pretty attached to me, I guess—that I just stayed on with them. They were like my parents.

Janet: What were they like?

Frank: They were pretty good to me. Gramps is eighty—but he's a great old guy. We still go fishing together—just like we always have. He's amazing.

Janet: When did your grandmother die?

Frank: Let me see—I was sixteen—1959. My grandfather lives with my aunt now, my mother's sister.

Janet: Where did you go when your grandmother died?

Frank: I moved in with my mother and Bert and their kids. It didn't really work very well—Bert was all right, but I was too old to get used to living there and taking orders from him.

Janet: Yes. That would be hard for a sixteen-year-old.

Frank: Boy, it was—I left as soon as I was old enough to go into the service—didn't even graduate from high school—but finished up while I was in . . .

Janet: Where were you in the service?

Frank: I was in Viet Nam—but early, so I didn't get into much. I was back and finished my tour before things really got bad over there.

Mary: It's strange—I was just thinking Frank's mother didn't raise him—most of his life—yet they're closer, in a way, than she is with the other two, Frank's half brother and sister.

Frank: That's sort of true, I guess. They both moved away. Al lives in Saint Louis—he's a teacher. Betty's married and lives in Chicago—so I'm the only one near. And Bert died five years ago—so Mom lives alone—although her sister and my grandfather are not far away.

Janet: Does your mother work?

Frank: Oh, yes, she's worked for Morris's department store for about thirty years, off and on. She started out really as a domestic doing cleaning and stuff. Then she moved into stock. Now she does a lot of inventory work, still connected with stock, it's a pretty good job. She's always had a lot of—I don't know—push or guts. Drive, I guess, is the word. O.K., Mary, now it's your turn. I'm doing all the talking.

Mary: O.K. Let me see, I was born on June 15, 1946—in Dayton. I wasn't there long, 'till I was about three. Then we moved to Cleveland when my father got his church.

Janet: Your father's a minister?

Mary: Yes, Baptist. He retired in 1974 after twenty-five years with the same church. My parents were older than Frank's. My father's seventy. They had us pretty late.

Janet: What about your mother?

Mary: Mother died almost seven years ago in 1971—of cancer. It's been a hard time for Dad—for all of us.

Janet: You mean losing your mother?

Mary: Yes—that—and my brother and everything. My brother was killed in a motorcycle accident three years ago. But it was even more than that. It's sort of a long story.

Frank: Why don't you tell her about it?

Mary: Well, I guess it is all very important in my family. There were three of us—and my brother was the youngest—and the apple of my father's eye. He had so many dreams for Eddie—he wanted him to go into the university. But I guess it was that minister's son business. He was kind of wild as a kid. Not really, but by my parents' standards he was!

Anyway, he did finish high school. And started college, but the next thing we knew, he'd dropped out of school. He was living with a girl, a girl my parents didn't approve of, and they weren't married. It really broke my father's heart. They had a terrible row, and Eddie took off to the West Coast. We didn't hear too much about them.

They got married and had a little boy, Jeff. He's about four now. Not too long after that, Eddie was killed. That made it much worse for my father—to have him die when there were such hard feelings—they would have made up, I'm sure—Dad felt better after they married.

Janet: Has there been any contact with his wife or the child?

Mary: No. I heard she's moved back to Michigan. Her mother's here. I guess my father sounds—sort of stiff-necked—I guess he is. But the church and religion were his life. He's really a marvelous man. He was born in real poverty and got himself to college—a small religious school in Alabama—worked his way through.

He was so respected in the community. His church was the largest black church in Cleveland. That put a lot of pressure on him, and our family was always in a fish bowl.

Janet: That's a lot of responsibility to head a large congregation like that. But your father's really had a lot of losses, hasn't he?

Mary: Yes. It's been hard times for us all. Daddy has his faith—and I have Frank and the kids—that's what gets us through, I guess.

At this point, the couple talk about the difficult time the family has been through. Mary talks about the telephone call in the middle of the night that told her of her brother's death. She speaks of the pain of having to tell her father and becomes tearful as she talks about it. Throughout, Frank shares her feelings and comforts her by taking her hand.

After some time, they seem ready to return to the genogram.

Janet: When were you two married?

Mary: June 12, 1967.

Janet: Was that the first marriage for both of you?

Mary: No, I was married before—right out of high school.

Janet: When was that?

Mary: 1962. We separated in less than a year. We were just kids. (Mary became quite anxious at this point.) Will that make a difference—I mean about our being able to adopt?

Janet: Absolutely not. It's how things are going for you now that's important—in terms of what adoption might mean to you—or what you bring to it. For instance, Frank, you know what it means not to be raised by your biological parents.

Frank: Yeah—I didn't think about that—sort of like a boy we'd adopt—and I know what it's like not to know your parents. I only saw my father a few times—he went back out West. He lives in San Mateo. In fact, I've been thinking of getting in touch with him again, it's been a long time.

Mary: In fact, we've been thinking of taking a trip out there some time. That sounds like a good idea, now. . . .

Frank and Mary stop here to talk about Frank's father, and their plans to visit him and their wish for their children to know their grandfather. Frank mentions his regret at being cut off, not only from his father, but from all of his father's family. They then return to working on the genogram.

Janet: Let's add your children to the genogram. Beth was born when?

Mary: May 11, 1968. Her name is Elizabeth Ryder. Ryder was my maiden name. And Ann—her name is Mary Ann—was born in December, 1971. They were both born in Detroit.

Janet: Have you had any other pregnancies?

Mary: Yes, I had a miscarriage between the two girls. In my first marriage I had a boy who died at three days. He had a heart defect.

Janet: What was his name?

Mary: (Looking startled) Robert, Robert George, after his father and my father.

Frank: Gee, I never knew that. I mean, I knew about the baby, but I never knew his name.

(Both sit quietly for a minute, seemingly lost in thought.)

Mary: It was a long time ago. He'd be big now—sixteen. It still makes me feel sad. I think that's one thing that finished our marriage. We were such kids and instead of being able to help each other with the loss, we just moved farther apart.
        (Turning to Frank) I'm sorry, hon, do you mind my talking about it?

Frank: No, I'm glad. I've always wondered about it, but just didn't ask.

Janet: That's really one of the things about doing a genogram. It often helps people to be able to talk about things.

Mary: I can see that. I look at this and see all those losses—both Frank and I have lost a lot of people when you think about it.

Janet: This may have something to do with your wanting to adopt—particularly a boy, I don't know—but it's something you may want to think about.

(Frank and Mary are quiet for a while.)

Mary: Funny, I was thinking about little Jeff, my brother's boy—wonder how he's doing.

Janet: Yes, I would think you would think about him often.

After some discussion of Jeff and the possibility of contacting his mother and healing this breach, Mary and Frank return to the completion of the genogram, adding a few more facts—birth dates, occupations, and similar information.

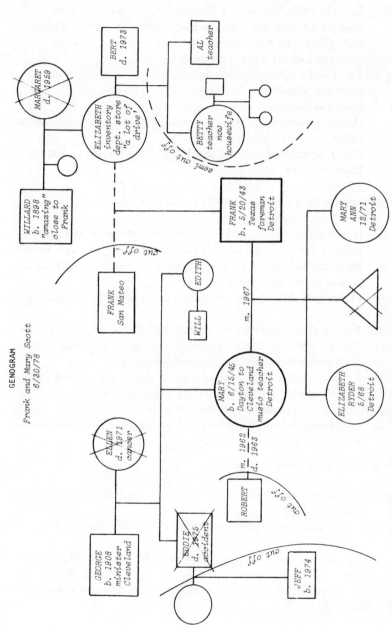

Figure 5.1 GENOGRAM—FRANK AND MARY SCOTT

ANALYSIS OF THE GENOGRAM

The interview with the genogram surfaced much that may have relevance to this couple's wish to adopt a son, and gives evidence of the special life experience each has had that may give particular meaning to adoptive parenthood. Figure 5.1 shows the Scotts' genogram.

Frank had been raised by grandparents and could well have strong feelings of kinship with a boy going through a similar experience. He had been estranged from his father which has some bearing on his feelings in assuming the role of a father to a son. Further, he was unable in his adolescence to take on his stepfather as a father.

Frank had three men who were fathers to him, but his grandfather seems to have provided him with fathering. One might speculate that he longs to be the father of a son, but also experiences some unsureness and uneasiness in thinking about assuming this role. He may wonder on some level whether a boy will allow him to be his father or whether he will be as he, Frank, was with his stepfather.

Mary approaches adoption with many losses that are only partially resolved. The loss of a baby boy in her first marriage continues to be a source of pain. Beginning to talk about it with Frank may help her better come to terms with that loss.

The loss of the brother was another tragedy and not the only a personal loss for Mary, because she also feels a great deal for her father who lost a son and a grandson through death and is alienated from his other grandson. A boy coming into this family may well have to carry a considerable burden if these losses are not more fully worked through. This genogram interview has not only aided in the family assessment, but it has also pointed the way to the next steps for the worker and the family in the adoption preparation process.

Chapter 6

INSIDE THE FAMILY SYSTEM

The EcoMap leads to an understanding of the family in its world, and the genogram pictures the development of the family system through time. The next task is to attempt to understand the family as a system and to be able to identify the major dynamics that operate within that system. By focusing on the family as a system, it will become apparent that much of the information gained through the examination of the EcoMap and genogram will be relevant to understanding the family system.

To the extent that the EcoMap portrays the family's exchanges with its environment, examination of the map relates to our discussion of the notion of "boundaries" around a family system. The EcoMap tells us a good deal about the extent to which the boundary around the family is open.

A discussion of the genogram tends to surface family norms about occupation, life style, and other accepted behaviors, and thus, provides a background for the discussion of the rules and values that govern the current family system.

The primary task in understanding the family as a system is to view the family, with its characteristics and its style and mode of function, as a whole. Frequently, when social workers attempt to understand families, they make individual assessments of each family member and add them together. Unfortunately, individual assessment of each family member does not produce an understanding of the family. Many of the salient characteristics of the family emerge out of transactional relationships among family members and can only be identified by viewing the family as a whole.

In attempting to understand a total family system, however, the complexity and multiplicity of variables is overwhelming. A verbal description of a family is not unlike listening to a radio announcer's description of a football game. Although the announcer may be able to describe the movement of the ball and the participation of two or three players, the rest of the action that has major impact on the fortunes of the ball is lost.

This chapter will present a way of looking at the family system by focusing on a few major characteristics of the family. The family is defined as a stable, open, rule-governed, regulatory system. From this definition, areas for assessment develop. First, the concept of an open, stable system is clarified. Then, the areas of assessment are discussed through exploration of the following questions:

(1) What is the nature of the boundary around the family and the boundaries between family members?

(2) What is the structure of the family relationship system?

(3) What is the nature of the family communication system?

(4) What are the family rules and roles?

(5) How is the family regulated?

The chapter ends with the presentation of two simulations which, like the EcoMap and the genogram, attempt to capture and objectify the family system. These are called "family sculpture" and "family diagramming."[1]

THE FAMILY AS A STABLE SYSTEM

Perhaps the best way to understand what is meant by the notion of the family as an open, stable system is through the use of a metaphor. For example, the dynamics involved in maintaining the body temperature at 98.6 degrees or the temperature in a house at a constant level provide useful illustrations.

The thermostat in a house may be set at 70 degrees. This is the stability or balance between heat and cold that the mechanism is set to maintain. It is a cold, windy day outside. No matter how well insulated, the house is semi-open, and cool drafts sneak under the windows and doors. The house cools off until the temperature reaches 68 degrees at which point, a communication is sent to the furnace that says, "turn on." The house then begins to warm up until it reaches 72 degrees at which point another message is sent to the furnace that says, "turn off." Temperatures below 68 degrees are defined as "too cold" and above 72 degrees as "too hot." These settings on the thermostat are the "rules."

A family may be understood in these terms. A simple example follows. A family consisting of two parents and thirteen, eleven, and eight-year-old boys has a rule about hair length. "Boys in our family keep their hair so that it does not reach the collar." When hair begins to reach that point, the family regulatory system that enforces the rules is set in motion. Parents send a message, "John, get your hair cut."

If John fails to do this, certain pressures are exerted. Father may ridicule, "You look absolutely awful," or threats may be used, "If you don't get your hair cut, you can't go with us to dinner and the movies because we don't want to be seen with you." That does it! John complies with the family rule and gets his hair cut.

However, a family is different from the body or the thermostat mechanism in a house because the rules must change through time as individuals within the family grow and change, and as the outside world becomes a different place. For example, let us imagine that long hair is very much the style in John's school and that boys with short hair like John are defined negatively. John leaves the family system, goes to school, and returns with a different notion concerning hair length. This begins a negotiation process that may well lead to some kind of readjustment of the family's definition of the appropriate length of hair. This kind of redefinition occurs as a result of two forces.

The boy is growing and beginning to test the boundaries of the family. He also is moving out of the family, developing relationships outside, and being exposed to new ideas and standards. He is bringing these new ideas back into the family. As a result, the family is required to make some sort of adaptation through which it maintains its integrity as a system, but allows individual members to change and grow. Perhaps, the hair discussion ends with, "O.K., you can let your hair grow but keep it clean and combed." Hopefully, the family may even get to the point of saying, "We have to admit it, your hair really looks nice."

In thinking with a family about adoption, it is important to consider the nature of the family rules, the regulatory system, and the likelihood that a child coming into their home will have been exposed to different rules and different regulatory methods. One of the most important issues revolves around the family's adaptive style. Is the family flexible enough to provide room for individual change while remaining sufficiently the same to provide coherence, stability, and continuity.

These issues are important for all families but have special significance for families considering adding a child to their family—will the family have a powerful need "to make the child like them" or will they be able to allow the child to be who he is and expand the definitions of the family to include this different person. This leads to an examination of family boundaries.

WHAT IS THE NATURE OF THE BOUNDARY AROUND THE FAMILY?

The boundary around a family is that invisible line that separates what is "inside" the family and what is "outside" the family. The boundary is symbolically marked in a variety of ways. It can be represented by a series of attitudes, behavioral prescriptions, and characteristics that define what is required to remain "inside" the family. In the example above of the boy with the long hair, a part of the family boundary was defined by the allowable hair length.

The family boundary tends to become obvious when it is in danger of being violated. For example, while all the boys in the family had very short hair, no one knew where the boundary of "too long" was located. When the one boy's hair approached that point and the regulatory system was set into motion, the argument about hair length made the boundary rule obvious to all.[2]

Families with adolescents experience this tension continuously as the children push against the boundaries in their effort to differentiate and establish their own ways of being and doing. Similar boundary tension is likely to arise through the adoption experience. It is possible that families may be quite unaware of their boundaries until they are tested by a new person coming into the home with different values, behaviors, and attitudes.

Even more important than the characteristics that mark *where* the boundary is located is the extent to which the boundary around the family system is open and flexible. For families to be able to change and grow, that boundary must be relatively open. Change takes place when family members are allowed to move outside the family system and to have important experiences and relationships outside the family that produce individual change. Then members are allowed to move back into the system bringing change with them. This process happens throughout the family's life, as for example, when a kindergarten child comes home and quotes the teacher as a higher authority, or when a young adult from a conservative family gets involved in radical political activities.

An open family boundary also allows people and ideas to enter the family system, thereby bringing about change. Families differ a great deal as to how much they allow people from the outside to become "one of the family." Some families have a number of close friends who are "as family"—who may even be called "aunt" and "uncle." Other families draw clear boundaries between insiders and outsiders so that even sons-in-law or daughters-in-law are never really part of the family.

An examination of the EcoMap can lead to some sense of the nature of the boundary around the family. Do individual family members have important connections outside the family? Is a member allowed to have a friend, an interest, or an activity that is different from and not necessarily shared by the family? Are there important people in the family's life space, people that are welcome to move in and out of the family system?

It is also important to know whether a boundary is there at all. Some family systems' boundaries are so open and so tenuously marked that the system almost ceases to be a system, but rather is an aggregate of individuals. The boundary around the family provides the sense of belonging, of sharing, of "weness" in the family. It provides a sense of security, stability, and continuity for the family through time.

The boundary is strengthened by affectional ties that keep people connected, and lead them to sacrifice some individual needs or aspirations for the sake of family solidarity and continuity. It is also marked by the multitude of family rules and prescriptions that define acceptable and appropriate behaviors for members of the families. These rules provide stability and direction. They mean that family members do not have to start from scratch to renogotiate every transaction that happens within the system.

No matter what the nature of the boundaries and what family rules tend to mark the boundary, it is important that these boundaries be clear. Confusion and double messages about the rules that form the boundaries leave family members unable to find the boundaries and uncertain as to what approved behavior is.

Different kinds of boundaries work for different families and the range of the ways families deal with boundaries is wide indeed. Figure 6.1 illustrates this range visually. At one extreme where there is almost no boundary, the members of the family suffer from alienation, rootlessness, a lack of belonging. At the other extreme where family boundaries are rigid and closed, family members are enmeshed, fixed, and unable to move out, grow, or change. Within these two extremes, however, are a wide range of family styles.

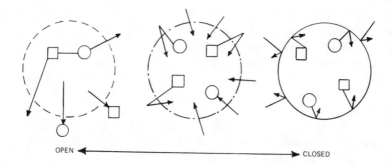

OPEN ⬅————————————————————➡ CLOSED

Figure 6.1 BOUNDARY RANGES

The nature of the boundary around the family has considerable relevance for decision-making around adoption. If a family has relatively closed boundaries and tends not to allow "outsiders" to become a part of the family, adopting a child, particularly an older one, could be painful and difficult. Out of their need such a family might adopt a child but might never really allow the child to belong.

Although there might be smooth periods of pseudo-belonging, considerable stress would develop for both child and family over anything about the child that might be different than the family's way. Sometimes such a family brings a child into its system only with complete denial of the child's connections and origin outside the family.

This kind of family would find a child's interest or concern about his or her origins extremely painful. A wish to maintain some contacts with his or her preadoption world would be terribly threatening to this family. The only way such an adoption can "work" is if the part of the child that existed and continues to exist outside the family is completely severed. This leaves the child divided, with a buried "secret self."

It is not unusual that relatively closed families apply to adopt in spite of the fact that the family style is incongruent to the adoption situation. Such families sometimes feel emotionally impoverished and alone behind their closed boundaries, and seek to fill their emptiness by bringing in a child. Such an attempt can only fail and lead to pain and disappointment for child and family

Families that tend to be located at the completely open end of the continuum shown in Figure 6.1 may not be able to offer the continuity, stability, and sense of belonging a child needs. They also are unlikely to have the network of emotional support required for taking on such a demanding task.

Finally, within this broad range, it is also possible to think about families with different kinds of boundaries for different child rearing tasks. For example, the needs of a family that tends toward the closed boundary end of the continuum may be congruent with a handicapped child with no ties who will always need considerable protection and care. A family moving more toward the open end of the continuum might be considered for a pair of early adolescent brothers who have been pretty much on their own and who need an emotional home base—but also require a lot of room and toleration of difference.

Before leaving the boundary issues, it is also important to gain an understanding of the family's style concerning the nature of the boundaries between members of the family. Once again, we are considering what is theoretically a continuum between no boundary at all to closed impermeable boundaries. On the one extreme where boundaries are not maintained between family members, we see families where there is no allowance made for personal or private space. Letters are read, people go through each other's drawers, and go into each other's rooms without knocking.

Members of these families tend to speak for each other as if they were able to be in the other's skin, in the other's head. At the other extreme are families in which members are closed to one another, in which no one hears, attends to, or can feel for the others. Closed boundaries lead to imperviousness, isolation, and alienation.

The range in family styles is wide. But for the enhancement of interpersonal functioning, it is important for family members to be open enough to one another, to be empathic while still respecting each other's rights to be separate. The dimension of interpersonal boundaries must be considered in terms of the developmental needs at different ages. It is necessary for the caretaker of a newborn infant to sense what the infant needs. The fusion between the newborn infant and the mother or substitute mother has survival value for the infant. However, as the child grows, the boundary between the child and parents grows, too. We smile when we hear a mother tell a grown man to wear his rubbers. She is still taking responsibility for his feet!

WHAT IS THE STRUCTURE OF THE FAMILY RELATIONSHIP SYSTEM?

Another approach to understanding the family is through identifying the structure of the family relationship system. Which family members are particularly close? Is there one member of the family who tends to be located in the center of the family? Is there one that is at the outer boundary? Is one member seen as supporting another? Is there a pair of siblings that relate very strongly to one another but less so to the rest of the family?

It is not easy to capture the dynamics of the family relationship system. They, too, are shifting and changing over time while still maintaining some sort of balance. The relationship structure of a family becomes more obvious in times of rapid change and crisis. For example, if the grandmother is in the home and occupies a central position in the relationship system, her placement in a nursing home will produce a major upheaval in the system. Everyone in the family will shift and change to form a new balance without her.

Will someone else move into the vacuum created by her leaving? If so, what effects will that person's shift have on others in the family? Since a system is a structure of interrelated parts, we know that a shift in one part of the system will reverberate throughout. Every part of the system will in some way be affected.

Just as the loss of a family member occasions major change, so does the addition of a family member. When a family adopts a child, the position of everyone in the family is altered. Even though the child is wanted and welcomed by every family member, the accompanying position shifts may cause discomfort. The family may tend to attempt to regain its old familiar balance. This attempt places considerable pressure on the new member.

Young children often demonstrate the effects of this shift very dramatically around the birth of a sibling. Part of them longs for the old family and their old position in it. Not infrequently do children suggest that the child be returned to the hospital.

WHAT IS THE NATURE OF THE FAMILY COMMUNICATION SYSTEM?

We have looked at the structure of the family system. The nature of internal and external boundaries have been described; the family relationship system has been discussed. Although the family as a communication system is very intimately related to the relationship system, a different level of phenomenon is observed.

The family structure may be likened to the system of telephone cables in a community. The communication system could be thought of as the number and content of the messages carried over the wires. The number of messages will, in part, replicate the relationship system as few messages will pass from family members to an isolate, and an over-involved pair will have many messages going back and forth.

It is also important to get a sense of the quality of a family's communication. This dimension of family operation is emphasized since it is through open communication that a family transmits feelings, ideas, and information. Clear, open communication keeps the boundaries of the family clear so that expectations are understandable. Clear, open, and active communication in the family is essential for adaptation and for family problem-solving. In achieving an understanding of a family's communication patterns and skills, the following question may be considered: Is there open communication about important issues throughout the nuclear family system and into relevant parts of the extended family system? The very way the family has shared the fact that they are considering adoption gives clues about the communication system. Early in the contact with the applicant(s), one may ask, "Who knows that you are considering adoption?", and "What do they think?" Answers to these questions surface the extent to which important issues effecting the total family are discussed with the members.

Other questions may illuminate the communication system. Are family members able to communicate their needs, hopes, fears, and concerns about taking this step of adopting a child? Are children listened to and are they validated? Do people talk for each other or do they allow members to speak for themselves? Are communications clear and unambivalent? Does nonverbal communication support or contradict verbal communication? Families vary a good deal in communication style. Workers must be careful not to evaluate the family's communications in relation to his or her stylistic preference. No matter what the style, the main question is, does this family's pattern of communication work for them in appropriate sharing, decision-making, and problem-solving?

WHAT ARE FAMILY RULES AND ROLES?

All families have rules. Earlier we defined the family as a rule-governed system. Rules provide the stability, commonality, and guidance family members require. They form the family "culture," the shared meanings, values, standards, patterns, and identifications that define the individual character of each family as different from all other families. Family rules belong to the family but are also often deeply affected by the cultural world within which the family has developed, and also by the family's experience through time and the themes that come to characterize the family.

Some of the issues that family rules are about have already been discussed. Although family structure was dealt with as a separate issue, the expectations and prescriptions that, in part, define the nature of the structure are family rules. Families have consistent rules over time about the nature of family boundaries and views of who is to be included in the family.

One family's rule may be: "All blood relatives no matter how distant the connection are within the boundary and all others are outside." Another family's rule about the boundary may be: "Only mother, father, children, and grandparents are really inside the family; all others are out." Still another family may have a rule that includes special names, friends of the family— "love aunts and uncles," as was discussed before.

Life events and exigencies affect the nature of boundaries. For example, during and after the major Jewish migrations to the United States from central and eastern Europe around the turn of the century, people who came from the same village were taken in "as family." The salience for the rules about boundaries for adoption has been discussed above.

Family rules that affect the structure of the relationship system may also be discovered through the genogram. For example, in one family the first-born daughter is defined as particularly close to the father and his family, while the second-born daughter has special closeness with the mother. Such rules have relevance for adoption in that they might define the special spot in the relationship system reserved for the adopted child. Perhaps the family is like the one described above, and the mother is asking for a second daughter.

The communication system is also regulated by family rules. The structure of communication processes are prescribed, as well as the content. Each family has rules about approved subjects, disapproved subjects, and family secrets. In thinking about family rules, the major issue is to identify those that have special relevance to the request to adopt. For example, if one subject the family cannot discuss is the death of a child they are now seeking to replace through adoption, this is extremely relevant.

Other questions about rules in families considering adoption concern whether it would be possible for an adopted child to obey the rules or fulfill the expectations that have major importance in a family. If the genogram surfaces a heavy emphasis on academic achievement, a child without the potential for high marks would be at odds with the family requirements. It might even be possible to construct a profile of a "typical" family member. "People in our family like to eat; aren't 'brains' but like to work hard with their hands; love the out-of-doors, are very interested in and close to family, and are physically strong."

An interesting discussion with a family could be around family rules, characteristics, and life style. Again, this is not an evaluative process. In no way is the worker making a judgment on whether the rules are good or bad. The worker is assessing what kind of child would fit into the family profile well enough to be able to belong.

RULES ABOUT ROLES

Another series of rules has to do with definitions of appropriate behavior for people occupying different roles in the family. However, great caution must be taken in considering role definitions as a part of family assessment. Role definitions are highly culture bound, and also have evolved as adaptations to the demands of living under different circumstances. Perhaps nowhere has sexism and racism impacted thinking about families more than in the development of notions of appropriate role behavior.

Consider the sexism in the following role definitions in a volume by Theodore Lidz, a widely read and highly influential psychiatrist.

The family is divided into two genders with differing and complementary functions and role allocations as well as anatomical differences. The feminine role derives from the woman's biological structure and is related to nurturance of children and maintenance of a home, leading to emphasis on interest in interpersonal relations and emotional harmony—an expressive affectional role. The male role is related to the support and protection of the family and leads to an emphasis on instrumental—adaptive leadership characteristics."[3]

Such culture-bound notions of the "ideal" or "healthy" family have had considerable influence on the assessment of families for adoption. They have tended to exclude families that have devised alternative role arrangements through different cultural values, different personal preferences or style, or the dictates of economic realities. Biased views of boundaries between the generational roles have also been rigidly drawn with clear distinction between the parental generation that guides, educates, and nurtures, and the child generation that is guided, educated, and nurtured.

Mental health professionals have been concerned about "pathological families" where a child takes over parental roles with siblings. This again is a highly culture-bound notion. Many cultures induct children into taking responsibility for younger siblings and for nurturing tasks.

In fact, the sharing of the parental role can be considered a source of strength and a highly adaptive response for many families. Another example of this kind of bias among professionals is found in the fact that continued reliance upon and involvement with the grandparent generation has often been negatively defined as a sign of immaturity and dependence on the part of the adults in the family. However, such intergenerational relationships are basic characteristics of the extended family form.

THINKING WITH FAMILIES ABOUT ROLES

In thinking about families and with families, it is important for workers to attempt to divest themselves of their own internalized picture of appropriate role arrangements in families. This is hard to do as these pictures tend to reflect not only one's own family experience, but also the constant reenforcement of stereotypical family forms that occurs through exposure to popular culture. We must all ask, "Does father really know best?"

How then do we think about roles? The major questions about role arrangements in families have to do with efficacy, clarity, flexibility and general satisfaction. Does the role arrangement *work* for the family? Do the family tasks get done to the family's satisfaction? The modern family is a fairly heavily burdened work system. One of the ways roles get distributed is in terms of sharing family tasks. In a single parent family where the parent is the breadwinner, the children frequently tend to take over more of the family work.

Are the role assignments in the family clear? As with any family role, clarity and lack of ambiguity is more important for family functioning than the specific set of role assignments. If one of the children in the family is expected to take over a parental role in the absence of the parent, this arrangement should be clear to all.

Are the role arrangements relatively flexible? The flexibility of role assignments means that when needed, different family members can take over part of other members' roles. Such flexibility enhances the family's adaptive capacity in the face of changing demands, loss, or crisis. Finally, is the family itself content with the role arrangements? Do the different family members gain gratification from the performance of their particular roles?

Thinking together with a family about role arrangements helps build a picture of how a family functions in its daily life. Such a discussion can lead to a consideration of how the introduction of a new member into the family will alter the role arrangements. What new tasks will emerge? How will these tasks be distributed? The family will also consider what other role adjustments and rearrangements will have to be made. Is the family ready to make these adjustments? Again, the very discussion and problem-solving that must take place around these specific and often very practical issues leads to enhanced understanding of the family as a functioning communication and relationship system.

RULES ABOUT RULES

Families also have a series of meta-rules, that is, rules about rules. These rules dictate how the family deals with all the other rules. For example, may the rules be talked about? Sometimes there is a fairly strong prohibition against looking at and discussing the family itself. The worker may experience the tension mounting in the family as he or she initiates this kind of discussion. Again, an attitude of interest and acceptance on the part of the worker will reassure the family. Other meta-rules concern how rules are enforced and how they can be changed. This leads to consideration of issues of power in the family.

HOW IS THE FAMILY REGULATED?

In addition to being rule-governed, the family is also a regulatory system. This implies the use of power in supporting and enforcing the rules, in regulating the behavior, and in marking and maintaining the boundaries in the family. Issues around power pertain to whom has power and how is it exercised. Power may be held by one or two people at which point those in authority force conformity on the other members of the group. In contrast, power may be distributed among all family members with conformity to group norms based on consensus.

Different families show a different balance between the amount of power vested in the parents or in one parent, and the amount of power that is distributed among all the family members. Cultural differences dictate different power arrangements as do the ages of the children. Families tend to evolve from major concentration of power in the hands of the adults in the family when children are very small, to a more consensual style of regulation as children move into adolescence.

This shift is never easy and much of the very natural developmental conflict that takes place between parents and adolescents is around the issue of power distribution. In thinking about power, it is important to include members of the extended family system. It may well be that the major power in the family is a grandparent.

In examining a family's regulatory system, it is also important to consider how power is used. What are considered to be the consequences if a family rule is broken? Disapproval, punishment, loss of love, or threatened or actual expulsion from the family are some of the ways families tend to regulate members.

Family regulatory styles have considerable relevance to adoption as adopted children are particularly vulnerable to threats of an expulsion. Too often, the adopted child is conditionally accepted in the family; that is his or her belonging to the family is conditional upon acceptable behavior.

This kind of situation speaks to a different type of commitment the parent may have to an adopted child than to a biological child. It is just the conditional nature of the child's acceptance into the family that causes him or her to act out to provoke expulsion.

As painful as leaving the home may be, children may well experience it as a relief. They feel that they have asserted their authority and taken charge of the situation. They escape the helpless and passive position implicit in conditional acceptance. Issues of regulation and commitment may be explored and discussed as part of the decision-making process. However, this area is one in which families often need particular help through postadoption services.

INSTRUCTIONS FOR FAMILY SCULPTURE

We have simulated the family in space through the EcoMap and the family in time through the genogram. There is no comparable simulation that can capture every aspect of the complexity inside the family system. However, the nature of the family relationship system may be portrayed in a very dramatic way through family sculpture. This technique, originating in the family therapy movement,[4] may be used by workers and families considering adoption not only to surface the relationship system but also to anticipate the impact of the movement of a child into the system.

Taken together with the EcoMap and the genogram sculpture adds a new dimension to the understanding of this powerful relationship system, and lends an immediacy to the assessment experience that may be highly productive in the joint assessment process.

Family sculpting is a deceptively simple exercise during which the sculptor portrays a family through the construction of a living picture. The sculpture may be formed using actual family members or other people may be used to portray them. The family member builds a sculpture of the family by placing each member, one at a time, in the "family space" in such a way that in the sculptor's view, the location, position, and stance typifies the person.

Each person is added to the system and placed in relation to the others, and in a position that characterizes him or her. This process is continued until the total family has been placed. As much as possible, the placement is done nonverbally, although the sculptor may give brief directions to the family members to facilitate exact positioning. The sculptor may continue to make adjustments until the sculpture matches his or her picture of the family relationship system.

Family sculpture may be used with a potential adoptive family to gain a shared understanding of the relationship system, to see where the family feels they would place a new member of the family, and to anticipate the shifts that could occur. The effort is not to evaluate the relationship system but to help work and family experience the system and experience the placement of a child.

Although family sculpting sessions may take many forms, the following procedure is a format for use with a potential adoptive family:

(1) The sculpture session should follow the work on the EcoMap and genogram. By this time, there has been considerable sharing. Worker and adoptive applicants should be comfortable together and have developed a trusting relationship. The sculpture session is a good opportunity to involve the total family and is useful primarily in families larger than a marital pair.

Children enjoy sculpting sessions and often like to be the sculptor. Through the sculpture session, children in the family have an opportunity to share their responses to the idea of enlarging the family and can begin to anticipate what it will be like to have another child in the family.

(2) The worker begins by giving a simple explanation of family sculpture as a way for everyone to share together how the family seems to be arranged, and to experience how the family might change with the placement of a child. It is important to emphasize that every family is different. The family should not have the feeling that the sculpture is a way of assessing *whether* the family should have a child but rather to experience together how it would be.

(3) The worker then either asks who would like to do the sculpture or asks one member to start. He or she gives simple instructions on how to proceed, emphasizing that it should be nonverbal. The worker may suggest that the sculptors might imagine themselves at home in the evening. Where would people be? What would they be doing? Chairs or other props may be used. Placement of the members should include not only where they are in relation to all the other members but also where they are looking, how their bodies are positioned, and similar information.

(4) As the sculptor builds the picture, members of the family may well object because they see themselves and the system somewhat differently. For example, if a child puts Dad over in the corner behind a newspaper, he may not like the picture of himself nor what his son or daughter is communicating through the sculpture. *It is important to allow the sculptor to finish without interruption,* and to assure other family members that they will have their chance later.

(5) Once the sculpture is completed to the satisfaction of the sculptor and he or she has placed him or herself in the sculpture, the worker then "places" the "child," asking the sculptor where the child should go. A staff member should be alerted before the session to be available. This person should be, if possible, of the same sex as the child the family has requested.

   If the family has not made a request in terms of sex, it is useful to ask a staff member of the opposite sex than that of the worker to help. This allows the family to see how a male and then how a female fits into their system.

(6) At this point, it is useful to get feedback from all of the participants while they maintain their positions in the sculpture. Each member is asked how they experience where they are and particularly, how they experience the entry of the child into the family. It is important to get feedback from the "adopted child" in terms of how he or she experiences the family.

   Another family member may have a strong need to sculpt the family in a different way. If so, the exercise should be repeated from the other family member's point of view. Each perception brings new light on the family and the sharing of contrasting views facilitates communication.

The sculpture usually leads to a lively discussion about the family or about where the child ought to be placed. Discussion and different views of the child's potential place in the relationship system tend to surface the needs that each family member hopes the child will meet. Family sculpture is particularly useful in surfacing the feelings held by the children in the family about the plan to adopt. Such feelings may not otherwise be exposed verbally.

In one family consisting of two boys, the parents, and a grandfather in the home, the couple expressed interest in adopting a girl. The mother who built the sculpture placed the "stand in" for a girl they might adopt right next to her, demonstrating her wish for a relationship with another female in this very male family.

The youngest boy then took over and moved the "adopted girl" out to the boundary of the family, thereby reinstating his close pairing with his mother. His reluctance and fear about a girl coming into the home was thus objectified in the sculpture and was available for discussion.

One might imagine that should the Singer family do a sculpture, Marge would want to put the "adopted boy" near Dee, out of their concern for his isolation. In the session, however, Dee may have an opportunity to reflect back that he feels a little uneasy and perhaps a little crowded by what his parents perceive as "companionship."

FAMILY SCULPTURE IN STAFF MEETINGS

Although the most dramatic and most effective use of sculpture occurs when family members sculpt themselves, the use of this technique may facilitate understanding of families in other ways, too. When the staff in an adoption agency meets to participate in exploring different options in planning placement, the worker may present the family through sculpture.

Using staff members as "stand ins" for family members, the worker can build the sculpture and get feedback from the actors concerning how they experience their location in the family system. Further, the worker can try placing a child and tap the actor's responses to the shift in the system. Although such an exercise will not produce an exact mirror of the family relationship system, it can be suggestive and can serve as a thinking tool for worker and staff.

LEARNING TO SCULPT

Social workers tend to rely almost entirely on verbal communications and the written word in working with people or in expressing their ideas. It is not easy to shift to different modes of expression. The EcoMap and genogram demand that the worker move from total reliance on words to the use of paper and pencil simulations.

Staff, in wanting to learn these tools, practice on themselves and each other to gain a sense of comfort and mastery. Almost universally, workers have found that self-consciousness about the tools was related to their own changing role, and that clients took the use of the tools for granted and found them useful and interesting.

Family sculpture departs even farther from the social worker's usual work pattern. Workers need an opportunity to practice sculpture before they can be expected to use it with their clients. Staff groups can learn sculpture together. It is very useful if a worker volunteers to sculpt his or her own family, particularly at some point in the past. This makes the sculpture very real to the group as they begin to get in touch with the power of the family emotional system. Once one worker has completed a sculpture, others in the group are usually eager to sculpt their own families.

The use of sculpture in staff meetings is important, and as it becomes an accepted and practiced way of communicating and understanding a family, workers are comfortable to begin to use sculpture with adoptive families. The richness of the experience for all involved supports the further use of the technique by the worker.

FAMILY DIAGRAMMING

The family relationship system, once it is understood, may also be diagrammed by the worker, or an adoptive applicant and the worker can do the diagram together. Although diagramming does not have the impact or the richness of sculpture, it can be a conceptual aid in viewing the family as a total system. Extended family members who have important linkages into the nuclear family emotional system can and should be included in the diagram.

There are many ways to diagram families but the following system grows out of the EcoMap, the genogram, and family sculpture, and thus is explained here.

As in the EcoMap and genogram, squares are used for males and circles for females. First names and ages should be added for identification. The same code for signifying relationships may be used as is done in the EcoMap: a solid line for a strong positive connection, a broken line for a tenuous connection, and a hatched line for a conflicted connection.

Just as in the EcoMap, arrows may be used to indicate the direction of attention and investment. Boundary issues in the family can be depicted in several ways. For example, a mother and child who are fused or between whom there is insufficient boundary can be depicted as overlapping. Fusion or over-involvement may be shown by two or three heavy parallel lines. A family isolate may be depicted by making a bolder boundary around him or her.

Finally, as in the sculpture, physical space is used as the metaphor, through which to depict emotional closeness or distance in the relationship system. Therefore, the easiest way to diagram a family is to get a visual image of how they all would be placed in a sculpture. Once that mental picture is clear, it is then possible to begin to draw the family on paper.

As an illustration, the Singer family may be diagrammed as in Figure 6.2.

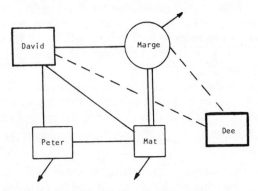

Figure 6.2 FAMILY DIAGRAM—SINGER FAMILY

NOTES

1. For an extensive discussion of the operation of the family as a system see Eleanor S. Wertheim, "Family Unit Therapy and the Science and Typology of Family Systems," Family Process 12:4 (December 1973), pp. 361-376.

2. This system operation has been described by Kai Erikson as the boundary maintenance function of deviance. See Kai Erikson, "Notes on the Sociology of Deviance," pp. 9-15 in Howard S. Becker (ed.), The Other Side. Glencoe, Ill.: Free Press, 1964.

3. Theodore Lidz, The Family and Human Adoptions, New York: International Universities Press, 1963, p. 53.

4. Frederick Duhl, David Kantor, and Bunny Duhl, "Learning, Space, and Action in Family Therapy," pp. 47-64 in Donald Black (ed.), Techniques of Family Psychotherapy a Primer. New York: Grune and Stratton, 1973.

Chapter 7

BEYOND ASSESSMENT

The goal of the family assessment process is to help workers and adoptive applicants move to an enhanced understanding of the family. Out of this process and understanding can come a shared awareness of the meaning to the family of the request to adopt, the needs that lead the family to consider this step, and the expectations the family may have of the adoption experience. The assessment process identifies the resources available for help and support in taking on the demanding tasks involved in the adoption of a child with special needs.

THE FAMILY ASSESSMENT PROCESS
AND DECISION-MAKING

In the past, the home study has been used by the worker to evaluate and to rule families "in" as acceptable or "out" as not acceptable. The emphasis in the process, described in this volume, is on a shared educational process that can result in the discovery of what kind of plan or what child would best fit the family's needs, style, and expectations.

The joint assessment process is a change process in that, as the adoptive applicants learn more about themselves and their families and the meaning of their request to adopt, they may reevaluate some of their expectations and realize that they must seek other ways to meet certain needs.

The change process that is stimulated by joint assessment may lead the applicants to withdraw their application out of a realization that the problem to be solved or the need to be met can be better handled in another way. For example, in doing an EcoMap with one couple, it became apparent that the husband was deeply involved in a variety of demanding but rewarding activities outside the home. Looking further at the family, the two boys, ten and twelve, were also active and involved. The wife had almost no rewarding transactions in her life. The marital pair shared very little. The EcoMap surfaced the loneliness and increased isolation of the wife and the growing estrangement in the marriage. The wife was seeking another child to fill the void. The husband was supporting her request in hopes that it would keep her occupied and off his back.

Early in the assessment process, the couple decided that adoption was not the answer to their marital problems and the wife's growing feelings of uselessness. They accepted a referral to a marriage counseling agency with the understanding that they could reopen their application in the future, if they decided they wanted to pursue it.

The change process stimulated by shared assessment may also lead to alterations in the system that prepares the family for adoption. For example, in the Scott case, the genogram reported in detail in Chapter 5, surfaced losses that had been very painful for Mary Scott and her hope that a child would somehow ease the pain through replacing the lost, loved family members. The discussion of the losses reawakened the incompleted mourning process.

Mary had been aware of her deep feelings and continued sadness around the loss of the child from her first marriage. The sharing of this in her present marriage allowed Mary to better deal with the mourning that she had been unable to discuss with her husband. Further, the discussion about the loss of her brother started another process. She began to question the break between her family and her dead brother's wife and child. Mary reevaluated the family bitterness toward the wife and reached out to her sister-in-law.

This reconciliation of Mary and her sister-in-law eventually led to a healing of the rupture between Mary's father and the brother's wife. This allowed him to establish a relationship with his grandson. In other words, one lost child was mourned while the other was reunited with the family. The Scott family was then able to adopt a son, a boy who could be himself and who did not have to carry the burden of the family's losses.

On rare occasions, adoptive applicants and workers may complete the shared assessment process with differing views about the next steps. The worker may feel that the needs the family brings to the agency cannot be met through adoption, or that the family does not have a resource network to support the care and nurture of a child. The applicants, on the other hand, do not agree.   The ultimate responsibility for the child in the agency's care is in the hands of the worker and the agency. The worker must act in the best interests of the child. However, the welfare of the applicant is also of concern to the worker and agency. It is the worker's aim to protect the family from the pain, frustration, feelings of disappointment, and failure that accompany an adoptive placement that does not work out.

When this differing view of the appropriate decision emerges through the joint assessment process, the worker's opinion is based on his or her knowledge of the family, its needs, expectations, and style. The worker can say with conviction and honesty, "It just won't work." The judgment is not based on the view of a family as "good" or "bad," as "functional" or "dysfunctional", but simply on a prediction that for this family, adoption would not work.

The special requirements for success in being adoptive parents, particularly adoptive parents of children with special needs, are not necessarily the same as for biological parenting. The worker, in taking a position different from the applicants', must be honest in explaining why he or she feels it "won't work." For example, a family with rather firm, closed boundaries, strong cohesiveness, and very definite prescriptions about what their children should be like, showed throughout the assessment process that they were comfortable with similarities and uncomfortable with differences.

The "differences" of an adopted child, it was felt, would be a stumbling block to the integration of the child into the family. He could not remain different and belong. The family would have a need to deny his difference which would leave him feeling, on some level, rootless and discounted.

The worker was honest in describing why she felt adoption would not work, in no way criticizing the close, cohesive family style, but simply taking the position that adoption for such a family is painful and disappointing. The family demonstrated exactly what the worker meant in the assessment by being unwilling to hear what the worker was saying, and being unable to tolerate the worker's different view of the situation.

PREPARATION FOR ADOPTION

The shared assessment process can lead to some very specific planning on how a family can prepare for adoption and for the adoption of a specific child. There are several kinds of preparation that may take place.

From the day the applicants approach the agency they should come prepared to learn more about adoption, about children with special needs, and about the special needs of all adopted children. This learning process should continue on through the assessment process. For many years, social agencies seemed to build their adoption program and service on the view that adoption was the same as having a biological child. This denial of difference deprived the parents of the opportunity to understand and to prepare for what was different about adoption and adoptive parenting.

There are two differences. First, the child was born of other parents and of a different biological heritage. He or she has two genograms and his or her identity is rooted in two families, the biological family and the adoptive family. The use of the genogram in the assessment process tends to connect people with the power and importance of biological roots, and leads to a discussion and recognition of the significance of the child's biological family to identity and sense of self.

If the adoptive applicants are able to truly accept the fact that an adopted child has two families, they are well on the way to being prepared to accept, understand, and help a child deal with his or her strong interest and concern about his or her biological heritage. Some agencies are using genograms with bio-families to gather information for children who are being released for adoption. This full family history is then available for the adoptive family and child.

Second, the adopted child also has had some life experience and some history before going into adoption. Adoption practice has attempted to keep this to a minimum by placing children, hopefully, right from the hospital. This means that although the child had different biological roots, his or her life experience starts with the new family. However, the vast majority of children available for adoption today are older children who have had considerable life experience prior to adoption. Adoption should not represent a break in the life line of the child. The adoptive family and child need help in integrating his or her life before adoption with life after adoption.

Adoption workers working with children who have experienced a series of losses and changes prior to adoption have made creative use of scrapbooks that contain the biography of a child[1] in words, mementos, and pictures. These scrapbooks go with a child into the adoptive home so that adoptive parents may share the scrapbook with the child and demonstrate acceptance of an interest in the child before, as well as after, adoption.

Continued relationships with important people in the preadoption life of a child also form a bridge between the two lives and save the child from experiencing more loss. In the past, agency concern about any contact between the biological family and the adoptive family led to a complete severing of any connection with the past life. Agencies feared that the biological family would learn the whereabouts of the child. Not only were all links to the biological family severed, but often contact with the former foster parents and friends was prohibited or strongly discouraged. This multiplied the losses experienced by the child.

These concerns, fears, and practice decisions are now being actively questioned by social workers, adoptees, and biological and adoptive parents.[2] Many are wondering if we have the right to deprive children of the sources of identity and strength that may exist in the biological family. Alternative adoptive arrangements are being explored, arrangements reflecting the reality that an adopted child has two families.[3] Such arrangements, in general, allow the adopted child to maintain some level of connection with his preadoption life and with his biological family.

It is beyond the scope of this discussion to present or explore these issues. However, they are highly relevant for assessment and work with the adoptive family. A part of the assessment and preparation process should include a discussion of these issues, and an exploration of how the parents might feel if their adopted child maintained contact with a biological grandmother or the former foster home. Such discussions define the nature of the family boundaries. They also make concrete the family's ability to accept and deal with the reality of the adoption situation.

We have emphasized the psychological and emotional aspects of preparation for adoption. The assessment process also forms a basis for some of the practical plans and arrangements that must be made, particularly for a child with special needs. The worker and family must identify together the resources that must be located and mobilized to meet these special needs.

The EcoMap lends itself very well to a discussion of the resources that must be found and the connections that must be developed. Are there special health care needs? Where can these needs be met? Are there special educational needs? Adding the child to the EcoMap and then locating the resources that must now become a part of the family's life space will demonstrate, in a concrete way, the increased complexity resulting from the child's joining the family and help needed in planning and preparation.

POSTADOPTION SERVICES

The shared assessment and preparation process also forms the basis for postadoption services that should be a regular part of all adoption programs. It should be assumed that adoptive families will have ongoing contact with the agency as different questions or problems arise.

In the past, the relationship between the adoption agency and the adoptive parents terminated with the finalization of the adoption. Often when parents later encountered problems, they were reluctant to return to the adoption agency as they felt that the emergence of a problem somehow signified their failure. Such parents sought help in social or community mental health agencies where they might or might not find a professional who had knowledge or experience in the special kind of problems to be solved or the tasks to be mastered in the adoption experience.

Adoption agencies, particularly those that are committed to the adoption of children with special needs are now moving to develop postadoption services. The shared assessment, preparation, and placement process develops a natural foundation on which to build such services. The agency knows the family and the child, and can join the family in problem-solving. Adoption agency staff can and should develop out of their experience a body of knowledge and skills basic to helping families with the special issues that may emerge.

The alternative forms of adoption, such as open adoption and shared parenting, that are now being considered make even greater demands on the adoptive parents, and they may well need on-going help and support in working out and maintaining these plans.

This volume presents a model of a joint assessment process that can take place between families making application to adopt a child and the adoption worker. The emphasis on the family assessment process grows out of the conviction that decisions and plans that have such momentous importance in the lives of people should be shared by those affected and should be based on knowledge and on understanding.

The primary focus here is on the use of the assessment process in placement planning. However, it is hoped that the assessment tools demonstrated and the understanding that may be gained about families will be equally useful throughout the total adoption process, including preparation, placement, supportive services, and postadoption services.

NOTES

1. Carol Williams, coordinator of Project CRAFT's sister project at the University of Southern California School of Social Work, has developed a film "The Scrapbook Experience" that utilizes this creative approach. The film is available from the Los Angeles Department of Social Services.

2. This literature is expanding at a considerable rate. See, for example, Florence Fisher, The Search for Anna Fisher, Greenwich, Conn.: Fawcett Publications, 1973; Mary Kathleen Benet, The Politics of Adoption, New York: Free Press, 1976; Betty Jean Lifton, Twice Born: Memoirs of an Adopted Daughter, New York: Penguin Books, 1977; Annette Baran, Reuben Pannar and Arthur D. Sorosky, "Adoptive Parents and the Sealed Record Controversy," Social Casework, 55:8 (November 1974), pp. 531-536.

3. See Annette Baran, Reuben Pannar, and Arthur D. Sorosky, "Open Adoption," Social Work, 21:2 (March, 1976) pp. 97-100; and Fernando Colon, "Family Ties in

Child Placement," Family Process, 17:3 (September, 1978), pp. 289-312. Also Joan Laird, "An Ecological Approach to Child Welfare: Issues of Family Identity and Continuity," in Carel Germain, People and Environments: An Ecological Perspective, New York, Columbia University Press, in press.

Chapter 8

TRAINING STAFF TO DO FAMILY ASSESSMENT

Those readers who wish to train others in one or more of the three assessment tools discussed in this volume may find the suggestions that follow helpful. Chapter 8 is divided into sections for the EcoMap, the genogram, and family sculpting. Each outlines a two to three hour training session. Each section includes a sample agenda; notes on contracting with trainees; the outline of a mini-lecture introducing the instructional activity; instructions for demonstrating the tool; instructions for one or two exercises; and suggestions for discussion and summary.

SAMPLE AGENDA

TIME	ACTIVITY
10 minutes	Contracting with the group
10 minutes	Mini-lecture: Introduction to the eco-logical Perspective
15 minutes	Demonstration: The How-to's of Ecomapping
45 minutes	Exercise 1: Do It Yourself
45 minutes	Exercise 2: The Singer Family
10 minutes	Summary

AUTHOR'S NOTE: Lynn Nybell of the Project CRAFT staff contributed greatly to the design of this chapter.

TRAINING OTHERS TO USE THE ECOMAP

TIME: 2 and 1/4 hours
MATERIALS NEEDED: A blackboard and chalk or newsprint and markers,
                                copies of blank EcoMaps and copies of the Singer
                                case from Chapter 4 for all participants.

CONTRACTING WITH THE GROUP

The leader should begin by reviewing the session agenda with the group
and describe briefly each of the major activities. In particular, it is important

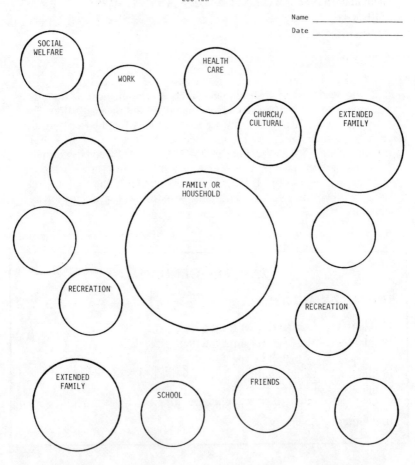

ECO-MAP

Name _____

Date _____

SOCIAL WELFARE

WORK

HEALTH CARE

CHURCH/ CULTURAL

EXTENDED FAMILY

FAMILY OR HOUSEHOLD

RECREATION

RECREATION

EXTENDED FAMILY

SCHOOL

FRIENDS

Fill in connections where they exist.
Indicate nature of connections with a descriptive word or by drawing different kinds of
   lines; ———— for strong, ------- for tenuous, ++++ for stressful.
Draw arrows along lines to signify flow of energy, resources etc. →→→
Identify significant people and fill in empty circles as needed.

Figure 8.1 ECOMAP

for the leader to note that there will be many opportunities for participation in the session. Participants will learn by doing. Assure the group members that they need only participate to the degree that they are comfortable. It is perfectly all right to participate by observing and by commenting on the exercises when they have been completed. Elicit any questions, reservations, or suggestions from the group members and establish a contract with them about their activities and roles during the session.

MINI-LECTURE: INTRODUCTION TO THE ECOLOGICAL PERSPECTIVE

The major points that should be included in this mini-lecture are summarized below. These points are drawn from Chapter 4. Study this material and then present it in your own style.

Summary of the mini-lecture points:

I The science of ecology is the study of the sensitive balance that exists between living things and their environments and of the ways in which this mutuality can be enhanced and maintained.

II It is possible to look at families ecologically.

    A   Families live in an environment that includes air, water, and food, but it also includes elaborate structures through which humans meet their needs.

        1. Work systems, welfare systems, churches, and schools are all examples of such structures.

        2. Families must maintain a relationship with these structures in order to survive and grow.

    B   The family must have two-way transactions with the environment.

        1. Needed supports, supplies, and stimulation must flow into the family.

        2. Family members must move out into the environment and find opportunities to develop.

    C   Families also have connections with the environment that are stressful and conflicted.

        1. Stress and conflict are part of the world of any living system.

        2. Some sort of balance between stressful and supportive connections must be achieved if the family is to survive and develop.

    D   In working with an adoptive family to assess its capacity to adopt a child, we can think of the family in light of its environment and the nurture it receives.

III In many ways, this perspective is "old wine in new bottles." Social workers have always focused on the "person in the situation." Ecomapping is one way of doing just that.

IV Opportunity for questions and discussion.

DEMONSTRATION: THE HOW-TO'S OF ECOMAPPING

This demonstration requires a large blackboard or newsprint and markers. Blank EcoMaps should be handed out to participants. A summary of the major points to be included in the demonstration is presented below.

I   What is an EcoMap?

   A. Looking at a family ecologically leads you to consider a mass of complex, interrelated information.

   B. The EcoMap is a map of a family in its environment. It conveys a lot of this kind of information in a simple way.

II   When do you use an EcoMap?

   A. The primary use of the EcoMap is as an interviewing tool. It may be used with an individual, a couple, or a total family.

   B. It can also be used as a tool to help workers think about a family. It is also a useful case recording device.

III   How do you construct an EcoMap?

   A. First, put a large circle in the middle. This represents the household.

   B. Then put people into the household; a male is represented by a square, a female by a circle.

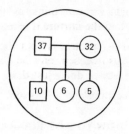

This is a family consisting of a father 37 and mother 32, a boy 10, and girls, 6 and 5.

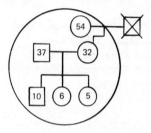

This is the same family, after the wife's widowed mother moved in after her husband died.

Here is a more complex household:

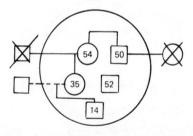

This is a household consisting of a single parent, divorced at 35, and her 14-year-old son. She shares a home with her widowed mother, her widowed uncle (her mother's brother), and an old family friend, unrelated, who has recently moved to the community and is living with the family.

C. Next, identify important aspects of the family's environment by asking about each of the systems in it: work, welfare, extended family, recreation, and so on.

D. Draw connective lines between the family and systems. These lines may connect with the family as a whole if they involve the total family or may be connected with specific individuals in the family.

E. The nature of the connection may be expressed in the type of line drawn. A solid or thick line may indicate an important or strong connection. A broken line may indicate a tenuous connection. A hatched line may indicate a stressful or conflicted relationship.

F. It is very useful to indicate the direction of the flow of resources, energy, or interest by drawing arrows along the connecting lines.

This is as far as you need to go at this time. It is not advisable to complete a total map at this point because to do so would be unnecessarily time-consuming, and in the end, repetitive. It is necessary only to demonstrate how the process takes place and how to get it started.

EXERCISE 1: DO IT YOURSELF

The best way to teach others to use an EcoMap is to get them to draw one themselves. The group should divide itself into pairs. One person in each pair is asked to draw the other's EcoMap. We have found that people usually enter into this activity with considerable interest. During the exercise the leader should be available to answer questions. After the exercise is completed, the leader should stimulate the group to evaluate the experience by asking several key discussion questions. During this evaluation period group members should be given the opportunity to raise questions and to make suggestions based on their experience. A number of discussion questions are suggested below. Those questions that we have found participants often ask are highlighted.

Discussion Questions:

1 Does anyone have any questions about the "mechanics" of Eco-mapping?

2 How did the people who drew the EcoMap experience the process?

3 How did the subjects experience it?

4 Did the subjects gain any altered sense of their life space?

5 How would you use Ecomapping in your practice? Can you think of a family you would want to use with it? When?

Questions Participants Often Ask:

Q. I found that I couldn't capture what my partner said about her relationships if I just used the "strong," "conflicted," or "tenuous" symbols. Is it okay to use other kinds of words or symbols to characterize relationships?

A. Sure! Some people like to write a word or two on the map that describes each connection. Others like to use different color pens.

Q. Should you carry around blank EcoMaps to use with clients? Or just use a blank piece of paper?

A. Each way has certain advantages. Starting without any structure may lead to somewhat greater flexibility. However, the use of the map saves time and quickly suggests to others what the procedure is about. Using the EcoMap may be an easier way to learn.

Q. My partner talked about relationships inside her family. Can you show that on an EcoMap?

A. Yes, but if you tried to do so I'm sure you found that what you can convey is pretty limited. The other tools we'll be looking at, the genogram, sculpting, and family diagramming, are generally richer ways of looking inside the family.

Q. I think this would be a good way to "show" a family to my supervisor or to my colleagues. Have EcoMaps been used in case conferences?

A. Yes. People have found lots of uses for them. They've been used quite a lot with the biological family of children in foster care. One worker designed an EcoMap for use with children.

EXERCISE 2: THE SINGER FAMILY

The Singer Family interview is included in Chapter 4. The interview text and the EcoMap that was produced during the interview should be made available to all the participants.

Three of the participants should be asked to read the roles of Marge Singer, David Singer, and Bill Dalton, the worker. We have never found it difficult to get volunteers. Afterward, members of the group should be encouraged to suggest hypotheses that they formed based on the interview and that they might wish to explore further with the Singers.

As the leader, you might wish to suggest some hypotheses in order to stimulate the process. "Bill Dalton's" hypotheses are summarized below.

— Marge was taking the lead in the interview and maybe in the interest in adoption.

— Marge seems to be the communicator in the family; the one who deals with interpersonal tasks.

— There seems to be a lot of demands on this family and minimum supports.

— Part of Marge's motive for wishing to adopt may be to make up to Dee for his "odd man out" status, and so he won't be a loner like his dad. She might also hope to deal with her own guilt about pursuing her own interests rather than having that "third" child.

— Marge is dealing with her needs through a lot of involvement with the outside world. Would a child with a lot of needs make her feel like the "walls were closing in"?

— Basic essentials, such as schools, income, housing, are all available.

SUMMARY

After completing the exercise, the leader should briefly review the ecological perspective and the way the EcoMap is used. The following summary points are suggested:

I   Taking an ecological perspective means looking at the family in the context of its relationships with other systems in its environment.

II   The EcoMap is a map of a family's relationships with systems in the environment.

A. The task of assessing an EcoMap can be shared by worker and family.

B. This assessment can lead to a discussion of the meaning of the family's request to adopt and to greater understanding of this request.

C. Filling out an EcoMap can help the family to identify resources that are available to support them if they adopt a child, as well as those resources they lack and need to develop if they prepare for adoption.

TRAINING OTHERS TO USE THE GENOGRAM

TIME: 2 hours
MATERIALS NEEDED: Blackboard and chalk, newsprint pads, a copy of the genogram interview with Frank and Mary Scott from Chapter 5, and a felt-tip pen for each participant.

SAMPLE AGENDA

TIME	ACTIVITY
10 minutes	Contracting with the group
15 minutes	Mini-lecture: Introduction to the genogram
10 minutes	Demonstration: The how-to's of genogramming
45 minutes	Exercise: The genogram interview with Frank and Mary Scott
20 minutes	Summary: The use of the genogram in adoption practice

CONTRACTING WITH THE GROUP

The leader should begin by reviewing the session agenda with the group and describe briefly each of the major activities. It is especially important for the leader to note that there will be many opportunities to learn by doing in the session through participation. Assure the group members, however, that they need only participate to the degree they are comfortable. Observing during any activity is perfectly all right so long as group members contribute to the evaluation of the activity and its utility for practice. The leader should elicit any questions, reservations, or suggestions from the group members prior to the start of the session and establish a contract with them about their activities and roles during the session.

MINI-LECTURE: INTRODUCTION TO THE GENOGRAM

The major points that should be included in this mini-lecture are summarized below. These points are drawn from Chapter 5. Study this material and present it in your own style.

Summary of the mini-lecture points:

I The EcoMap displays the family and its relationships with other people and systems in its life space.

II In addition to existing in space, families develop over time.

    A Each person is deeply rooted in his own family of orientation.

    B An individual's view of himself and of family are derived from his experience in his own family.

    C People tend to repeat in their current family what they experienced in the family in which they grew up.

    D Exploration of intergenerational family history with a family may lead to an understanding of why family members see the current family as incomplete or why they seek to build their family through adoption.

    E This exploration of family history may also surface expectations and role assignments that family members hold for a child who steps into a particular spot on the family tree.

III Opportunity for questions and discussion.

DEMONSTRATION: THE HOW-TO'S OF GENOGRAMMING

This demonstration requires a large blackboard and chalk, or a newsprint pad and marker. Again, a summary of the major points to be included in the demonstration is below.

I What is a genogram?

A. The genogram is a picture of a family through time. It makes the life history of a family over three or four generations available for observation.

B. It helps to surface naming patterns, major family events, occupations, losses, family migrations and dispersal, role assignments of family members.

C. A genogram also helps families feel the power and importance of their roots—which helps them appreciate the meaning of biological family roots to a child they would bring into their home.

II   How do you do a genogram?

A. Using basic symbols, a representation of the extended family system of any size or complexity can be constructed. These are the same symbols that are used in the EcoMap to depict the members of a household. The symbols are as follows:

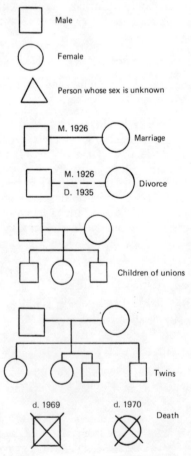

Three generations of a family might appear as follows:

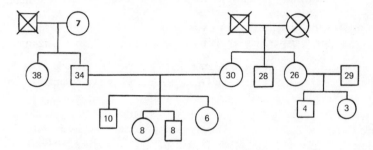

B. This serves as the skeleton to which information about the family can be added. Useful information includes:

Names: Identify family members and also show who in the family is named after whom.

Dates of Birth: Identify present ages and portray sibling positions within families. Further, dates of birth compared with other recorded dates indicate the ages at which the person was married, orphaned, became a parent, and so on.

Place of birth and current residence: Locates the family and tracks both family migration and family dispersal.

Dates of death: Not only portrays longevity but also surfaces family losses.

Cause of death: Surfaces family illnesses and family tragedies such as suicides, accidents, and so on.

Occupations: Demonstrates values, identifications, life style, talents and interests, and socioeconomic level.

Other personal characteristics: The following more subjective information may also be very important. The worker may ask what *role* a member occupied in the family. Also, it may be useful simply to ask the informant what word or two comes to mind when they think of that person. This kind of material gives character to the genogram and demonstrates recurrent family traits, patterns, and identifications.

Structural information: The genogram can also be used to exhibit some major structural characteristics of the family. Major communication patterns may be traced by connecting these parts of the family in frequent communication with a line.

Cut Offs: Indicate that some members or segments of the family are "cut off" and remote from others in the family system. These may be indicated by the drawing of a heavy line, boundary, or fence. Close groupings within the family may be enclosed with a broken line.

EXERCISE: GENOGRAM INTERVIEW
WITH FRANK AND MARY SCOTT

Distribute a copy of the genogram interview with Frank and Mary Scott and a felt pen to each participant. Divide the participants into small groups of three or four. Each small group should draw a genogram based on the interview. After the groups complete the genogram, ask the participants to think about the Scott family. The discussion questions below are intended as a guide. You may wish to replace them or to substitute others.

Discussion Questions:

1   What did the group members notice about the genogram in terms of significant events, patterns, and identifications?

2   What ideas do group members have about the possible meaning of the request to adopt?

3   What expectations might this family have for the adopted child?

4   What roles or identifications might the child be expected to assume?

5   How might you help this family become ready to adopt?

SUMMARY: THE USE OF THE GENOGRAM
IN ADOPTION PRACTICE

The preceding discussion of the Scott case should give the group a sense of how the genogram is used. The following summary points are suggested:

I   The genogram helps worker and family explore and understand the meaning of the wish to adopt.

   A. It may reveal why the family sees itself as incomplete or why it believes a child of a certain age or sex will complete the family.

   B. It may show whether adopting a child is an attempt to work through a loss or to repeat or replace a major relationship.

   C. It may show whether the request reflects a need of one of the marital pair or a need of each of them.

II   The genogram helps worker and family understand what role might be intended for the adopted child and what expectations and identifications the family may have for the child.

III This process of exploring the wish to adopt and the family's expectations of the adopted child my help families to identify needs they have that could burden the child. It can also help family members to think of other ways to deal with these needs so that the child is free to be himself.

TRAINING OTHERS TO USE SCULPTING

TIME: 2 hours
MATERIALS NEEDED: Blackboard and chalk or newsprint and markers.

SAMPLE AGENDA

TIME	ACTIVITY
10 minutes	Contracting with the group
10 minutes	Mini-lecture: The family relationship system
30 minutes	Demonstration: Family sculpting
50 minutes	Exercise: Family sculpting
20 minutes:	Summary: The use of family sculpting in adoption

CONTRACTING WITH THE GROUP

The leader should begin by reviewing the session agenda with the group, and describe briefly each of the major activities. It is important for the leader to note that there will be many opportunities to learn by doing by participation in the session. Assure group members that they need only participate to the degree that they are comfortable. Elicit any questions, reservations, or suggestions from the group members and establish a contract with them about their activities and roles during the session.

MINI-LECTURE: THE FAMILY RELATIONSHIP SYSTEM

The major points that should be included in this mini-lecture are summarized below. These are drawn from Chapter 6. Study this material and present it in your own style.

Summary of the mini-lecture points:

    I In addition to understanding a family's relationship with others in its environment and its development over time, it is useful to look at the family itself as a system and to identify major dynamics that operate within that system.

    II The complexity and multiplicity of variables in a family system is overwhelming. A few major characteristics are especially worth exploring. These include:

A   The nature of the boundary around the family and between family members. Is it quite open or semi-closed? Who is inside?

B   The structure of the relationship system in the family. Who is close to whom? What are the major triangles?

C   The nature of the communication system in the family. Who talks to whom about what and how?

D   The kind of rules that exist in the family. What is OK in this family? What is not?

E   The way the family is regulated. Who is the boss and how do the leaders use their power?

III The tool offered in this session cannot display all these characteristics. It is useful in portraying the family relationship system and often gives some indication of other characteristics.

IV Identifying the relationship structure in a family entails examining the following kinds of questions.

A   Which family members are close to each other? Which are distant from each other?

B   Which of the members seems to be located in the center of the family? Which is nearer the boundary?

V The family relationship structure will shift over time and, in particular, will experience a major change when a family member is lost or added. The adoption of a child will occasion such a change.

VI Opportunity for questions and discussion.

DEMONSTRATION: FAMILY SCULPTING

This demonstration requires a fairly large physical space in which to sculpt a family. Ideally, the participants should be asked to move their chairs into a large circle with plenty of room in the middle for the demonstration to take place. Key points in the process of demonstrating sculpting are described below.

I   Explain what family sculpture is.

A.   Family sculpture is a way of portraying the relationship structure in a family through the construction of a living sculpture.

1. A "sculptor" builds the sculpture by placing each family member, one at a time, in such a way that the location, position, and stance of that person typifies his relationship to the others.

2. The members of the family may be in the sculpture or other people may be used to represent them.

B.   Building a family sculpture with a potential adoptive family gives family members insight into the relationship structure in the family as it is and as it would be if a child were added.

II   Illustrate how to do a sculpture.

A.   At this point, indicate that you would like to sculpt a family with the group. It is important that you have a particular family in mind and have thought about how to sculpt it. If you choose to sculpt your own family as it existed at some point in the past, this makes the sculpture very real. It may also make it easier for others to learn by sculpturing their own families later in the session. However, you might wish to sculpt a case with which you are familiar. The Singer case from Chapter 4 of this book might also be used. It is a family with which all the participants in the training group will now be familiar.

B.   The leader, as sculptor, should select members of the group to represent members of the family. We have found that individuals in the group are occasionally reluctant to participate in the sculpture. It is not difficult to identify a person's reluctance through nonverbal cues. Try not to select a person who does not want to participate. You may wish to ask each person, "Are you willing to participate?" as you choose them. Or ask people to volunteer for each of the roles.

Family members should be placed one at a time. The sculptor should not speak as people are being placed and may have to remind the group members to be silent. Posture, position, physical closeness or separateness, eye contact or lack of it can all be nonverbally indicated by the sculptor.

C.   Once all family members have been selected or added, the sculptor surveys the sculpture and makes any adjustments he or she feels would add to it.

D.   Once the sculptor is finished, the group leader asks each person in the sculpture how he experiences his position in the family. Many participants in this process have clear and sometimes moving insights. The sculptor may wish to draw responses from participants about the comforts of the position they are in, the strains, the warmth, the limits, and so on.

E.   Others in the group may now be asked to offer observations about the family and particularly about its relationship structure.

EXERCISE: FAMILY SCULPTING

Practice is necessary if participants are to learn to use this tool in their work with clients. Such practice can begin in this session. After the leader has demonstrated the sculpting technique, the learning group should be divided into subgroups of eight or ten. Ask each subgroup to select one person to do the sculpture and one person to act as "monitor." The role of the monitor is to ask the participants in the sculpture how they experience their role and to ask the other group members for their observations. If time allows, others can take a turn as sculptor. The leader should be available to answer any questions or to consult with participants in the subgroups.

SUMMARY: THE USE OF FAMILY SCULPTURE IN ADOPTION

Sculpture is a new way of communicating for most social workers. In order to learn to use this tool, workers need to practice the sculpting of families so that they will be able to use this technique in presenting families on their caseload to each other.

We believe that the most dramatic and effective use of this tool is with potential adoptive families. During the training session, the leader should initiate a discussion of what it is like to use this tool directly with families.

Key discussion points are summarized below.

I   In working with clients such as potential adoptive families, the sculpture session should follow work on the EcoMap and genogram. Worker and family should be comfortable together before engaging in as emotionally laden an activity as family sculpting.

II   The sculpture session is most useful in families larger than the marital pair. Children enjoy sculpting and often like to be the sculptor.

III   The sculpture should not be used as a way of assessing *whether* the family should have a child but rather is a way of experiencing how it will be to have another child.

IV   In orienting a client family to the sculpting process, it might be helpful to suggest to the sculptor that he or she imagine the family at home in the evening. Where would different family members be? What would they be doing?

V   It is important to allow the sculptor to finish even if other family members begin to object or have other ideas. The other family members should be assured that they will have a chance to comment or to add to the sculpture after the sculptor has finished. If time permits and the other family members are interested, they can take turns at being the sculptor.

VI   Once family members are in place in the sculpture, the sculptor should be asked where he or she would place the adopted child. The worker or someone else can stand in for this child.

VII Family members should give feedback about how they experience where they are and how they felt about the placement of the adoptive child.

VIII If other family members wish to sculpt the family, the process should be repeated, and the differences in each sculptor's perceptions should be noted.

IX This tool is useful in surfacing needs that each family member hopes the child will meet, and feelings that each has about the plan to adopt.

REFERENCES

Attneave, C. (1976) "Social Networks as the Unit of Attention." In P.J. Gurin, Jr., M.D. (ed.), *Family Therapy*. New York: Gardner Press.

Averswald, E. (1973) "Families, Change, and The Ecological Perspective." In A. Ferber (ed.), *The Book of Family Therapy*. New York: Houghton Mifflin (Sentry Edition).

Duhl, F., Duhl, B. and Kantor, P. (1973) "Learning, Space and Action in Family Therapy: A Primer of Sculpture." In D. Bloch (ed.), *Techniques of Family Psychotherapy*. New York: Grune and Stratton.

Germain, C. (1973) "An Ecological Perspective in Casework Practice." *Social Casework*, 54,6(June): 323-330.

Guerin, P.J., Jr., M.D. and Pendagast, P. (1976) "Evaluation of Family Systems and the Genogram." In P.J. Guerin, Jr., M.D. (ed.), *Family Therapy*. New York: Gardner Press.

Papp, P. (1976) "Family Choreography." Pp. 465-479 in P.J. Guerin, Jr., M.D. (ed.), *Family Therapy*. New York: Gardner Press.

Papp, P., Silverstein, O. and Carter, E. (1973) "Family Sculpting in Preventive Work with Well Families." *Family Process*, 12.

Satin, V. (1972) *People Making*. Palo Alto, CA: Science and Behavior Books.

Simon, R. (1972) "Sculpting the Family." *Family Process*, 2: 49-51.

ABOUT THE AUTHOR

Ann Hartmann, DSW, ACSW, is Professor of Social Work at The University of Michigan and currently Director of Project CRAFT. She heads the Family Practice sequence at The University of Michigan and conducts workshops nationally in family assessment and intervention.